PERSONAL VALUES

The Application of Personal Values to the World of Work

PERSONAL VALUES

The Application of Personal Values to the World of Work

John M. "Chick" Stepahin

Pacific Press

Copyright © 2000 by John M. "Chick" Stepahin.

All rights reserved. No part of this publication may be used or reproduced, stored in a retrieval system, or transmitted in any forms or means, electronic, mechanical, photocopy, recording, or otherwise, without the prior written consent of the publisher.

Published by Pacific Press
P.O. Box 1965
Klamath Falls, Oregon 97601-0221
541.884.4818
FAX: 541.884.4818
E-mail: pacificpress@performancesolution.com

ISBN 0-9678526-0-9
Library of Congress Card Number: 00-190047

Edited by: Regina I. Stepahin

Printed in the United States of America

For information about purchasing this book for individual or corporate use contact Pacific Press.

Dedication

To Vergie

*Today's special moments are
Tomorrow's favorite memories...*

Contents

Preface – *Why? Why Not! Thank You!*. . . . . *i*

Chapter 1 – *It's About That Time, Huh?*. *1*

Chapter 2 – *Some Call It the Way They Want It* *15*

Chapter 3 – *Do as I Say, Not as I Do*. *29*

Chapter 4 – *Follow the Leader*. *43*

Chapter 5 – *The Generation Gap* *55*

Chapter 6 – *The Value of Diversity*. *69*

Chapter 7 – *Short Term Personal Gain and the
              Price of a Popsicle* *83*

Chapter 8 – *Taking Credit for Another Person's Work* *99*

Chapter 9 – *Team Player*. *113*

Chapter 10 – *Six Degrees of Connectivity*. *127*

Chapter 11 – *Status*. *141*

Chapter 12 – *Priorities*. *155*

Chapter 13 – *Procrastination* *169*

Chapter 14 – *The More You Know*. *183*

Chapter 15 – *Never Enough Time*. *197*

Chapter 16 – *I Value My Garden*. *211*

Epilogue *219*

Preface:

Why? Why Not? Thank You!

The value of life lies not in the length of days but in the use you make of them; he has lived for a long time who has little lived. Whether you have lived enough depends not on the number of your years but on your will.
Montaigne 1533-1592

Doubleday Dictionary defines the word *"preface"* as *a brief explanation to the reader at the beginning of a publication* and *Webster's Ninth New Collegiate Dictionary* defines it as *the introductory remarks of a speaker or author.* I've always been curious about how many readers conscientiously read the "Preface" to a book. Looking back on the many books and manuscripts I've read over the years, other than skimming the pages with italic numbers, I have to admit I've read very few "Prefaces." The few I've read and those I've quickly skimmed generally talk about the author's insights, why he wrote the book, then concluded with what seems like paragraph after paragraph, if not pages, of names of who contributed to his inspiration.

If you're like me, feel free to skip this preface and begin reading chapter one. I would not be insulted nor would I probably ever know you didn't read it, unless you told me. My story and what I want to say are found in the following chapters, not in this preface. But if you do decide to continue reading through this preface anyway, I'll attempt to provide a *"brief explanation"* and a few *"introductory remarks"* that might help set the stage and focus your thoughts for the rest of the book.

Notice the subtitle under the title "Preface," *Why? Why not! Thank You!*

First, let's address the *Why?* I'm proud to say that over the years I've been an observer, student of people, and specifically interested in their individual and collective behaviors. I'll intentionally avoid the academic and philosophical approaches to behavior by not getting into extensive detail (remember, a *Preface* is supposed to be brief) or trying to build a literary foundation based on all the different psychological theories of behavior and motivation. Theories and disciplines related to subjects like hierarchies of needs, behaviorism, conditioning, axiology, and all the other traditional and "neo" theories, is not the intent or purpose of this book. You don't even need an understanding of any of those theories and disciplines to read and appreciate this book. You just need a little experience in observing people and their behaviors.

What I've tried to do is tie or link individual and collective behavior with an individual's or an organization's beliefs and standards, which I refer to as *values*. Consistency and congruence between a person's personal values and his behaviors is most intriguing. Maybe I should say inconsistent and incongruent instead. In no way do I imply or intend to minimize academic and professional theories. My focus is on many of the everyday discrepancies between what a person says and does and what he believes, professes, or says is "important" to him. For me, awareness and being cognizant of our behaviors and how others interpret those behaviors, is extremely important.

A majority of the greatest and most influential historical, political, and religious leaders utilized stories as their primary way to get their messages across to others. Research backs up that fact. I have attempted the same "story" approach in this book, but without any visions of grandeur about personally being a great or influential leader. The stories are fictional in nature. The issues presented are very serious and based in reality, with a little bit of humor and sarcasm thrown in. The reality presented is seen through my eyes and based on over a half century of personal life experiences. My intent is to make you, the reader, a little more aware of your and others' behaviors, with reference to your values and value systems. Values and value systems manifest themselves through behavior.

As for the *Why not!* No, we're not in a Philosophy 101 or college logic class! I have a passion for trying to live up to my own personal values and value system(s). Notice I said, "trying." Unfortunately, I have to admit that I've fallen short in many situations. However, reflecting on and revisiting my own failures and observing what I consider discrepancies in *values* versus *behaviors* of friends, colleagues, acquaintances, and people in general, I hope this book can serve as a mirror for ourselves and a window for observation of others. No, there aren't any major revelations or prescriptive answers in this book (that will be the topic of a future book). Instead, it's hopefully a way for all of us to look at ourselves, revisit our own values and value systems, and continuously analyze our behaviors based on our own personal values.

Because a major part of our waking hours and personal identity revolves around our work and careers, the stories that follow center on work related situations that we can all identify with or have experienced ourselves. Personal values contribute to the set of values and overall culture of organizations as well, no matter whether they are incorporated as part of a company credo, mission statement or other framable document. Are we different people or do we behave differently at work versus how we behave outside of the work environment? That's also a topic for another book.

Finally, *Thank you!* I would like to extend my appreciation to everyone I've had the opportunity to meet, work with, talk with, argue with, disagree with, learn from, associate with, and observe over the years. You have all been an inspiration to me in the writing of this book! If some of the stories seem to "hit home," then I've done my job. In doing so, I hope I've contributed in some small way to your *values* of life.

As Montaigne wrote back in the 1500's, *"The value of life... depends not on the number of your years but on your will."*

We become better people, and a better society in general, by practicing "good" behaviors based on "good" values that comprise a solid value system.

*There is occasions and causes why and wherefore
in all things.*
                            Shakespeare 1564-1616

PERSONAL VALUES

*<u>Personal</u>: "Directly relating to a person's
character, conduct, personal affairs or
habits, etc."*
                            Doubleday Dictionary

*<u>Values</u>: "Principles or qualities
intrinsically valuable or desirable"*
                            Webster's Ninth New Collegiate Dictionary

Chapter I

It's About That Time, Huh?

*The innocent and the beautiful
Have no enemy but time.*
                    Yeats 1865-1939

"It's hard to believe that I've just passed the one year milestone, four more years to go till I'm fully vested and get an additional week's vacation," Bryan thought to himself as he turned off his computer at the end of a long day. No, let's make that a long week. What better time to look in retrospect at the past year and mentally summarize the year's highlights and accomplishments, similar to how the news media formats their annual *"Year in Perspective"* series between Christmas and New Year's Day.

Bryan officially accepted an offer for his position exactly three hundred seventy-two days ago. That number is important as you'll realize shortly. He joined one of the "premier growth companies" in the industry, or at least that's the way it was referred to and described in all the publications and financials he researched during the hiring and interview process.

Personal Values

"Premier Growth Company" was mild compared to what the company's web site boasted, not to mention how the company was presented to him by those he spoke with during the interview process. Somehow that hiring and assimilation process into the company seemed decades ago. Besides, in the last several years, according to the publications, the company was managing to produce good financials, with investment and dividend returns slightly above Wall Street's major indexes.

It's a wonderful sense of accomplishment, or possibly an adrenaline rush, to sit for the first time in your well-appointed "corporate" office, especially with a new employer. Notice that I used the word "corporate" as a descriptive for the office. I've spent my entire career in what would be considered "corporate" positions, so this present job change shouldn't be anything new, but somehow it was. At this company, I was frequently reminded that "corporate" has a connotation that implies power, success, achievement, independence, control, money, and all those other things a social caste system might want to attach to it. Even for what most people would consider minor and incidental tokens at other companies, here, they were elevated to comparatively unrealistic status levels. Come to think about it, before I even arrived for my first official day in the office, my name was already engraved on a nameplate and prominently displayed right beside my office door. What I thought at first was a brass nameplate embedded in a solid oak frame, eventually revealed itself as a gold spray-painted plastic nameplate engraved with my name "Bryan Mathews." Upon closer inspection, the engraving was more like the product of a homemade label-embossing machine. The original nameplate remains to this day even though I mentioned several times to the official corporate "Nameplate" manager, that my last name was misspelled. There's two "Ts" in my last name, not one. Early one morning during my second month at the office, I thought I would easily remove the nameplate and personally deliver it to the "Nameplate" manager. That was not to be when I discovered it was securely fastened to the wall-mounted simulated wood frame with double-sided tape and super glue. Oh well, so much for appearances.

The office did have an appeal about it, even though it was identical to most "corporate" offices in any other company throughout the country. You know, the large window that faces north with a view of nature at its finest. Finest in this case means one locust tree strategically positioned within an enclosed brick wall courtyard. One pre-cast concrete bench which might have blended in better at the local cemetery, an empty masonry birdbath perched on a pedestal, and various and sundry remains of attempts at landscaping finished off the view. Come to think of it, I can't recall if I ever saw anyone sitting on that concrete bench.

The large wide windows provided a wonderful daylight accent to the carefully chosen wallpaper, chair rail and carpeting. The office furniture appeared a little worn, but generally in good condition, definitely not brand-new or right off the Ethan Allen showroom floor. But on your first day, who cared? You probably remember your first day in "corporate" America the same way I do, more of a blur than anything. Think about it, walking into "Your" new office and lightly running your fingers over the furniture, stepping lightly on the carpet so as not to mess up the nap. You probably even looked up at the ceiling in awe for whatever reason, because it seemed only natural to do so as you surveyed your new environment.

Without wanting to appear overly impressed with yourself, just in case someone might suddenly come around the corner, the wonderful sensation of slowly sliding down into that high-backed executive chair, with its fully upholstered leather armrests, came quite naturally. What a sense of satisfaction and accomplishment, another adrenaline rush, when the chair totally embraces your body. After carefully adjusting the chair

Personal Values

to fit the exact height of your knees and proper back alignment, the sensation of finally leaning back with your hands folded behind your neck seems to create a moment, if ever so slight, of visionary speculation. On your mind's picture screen you can see yourself at the helm of your department's operations. There you are, leading, guiding, inspiring, mentoring, and all those other managerial and executive duties anyone would fantasize about on his first day in a new corporate job.

Just as I was about to be nominated to the post of Chairman of the Board in my mind's imaginary cinema, my vision was suddenly interrupted by a light tapping on the door. Did you ever wonder why people knock on a door that's wide open, which mine was? Already standing partially in my office was the "corporate" manager from the office one door down from mine. I didn't have the opportunity to meet her during the hiring and interviewing process, so I couldn't greet her by name. She entered my office with a wide smile, which seemed a little forced, and introduced herself as Mrs. Williams. Being that we were going to be corporate neighbors she granted me the permission to call her by just her first name, Heather. Her appearance in my doorway reminded me of the first cake-bearing neighbor who visits before the moving truck is completely unloaded. You know the type. Seems her intentions are focused more toward getting a head start on the neighborhood gossip circuit. Could Heather be the self-appointed corporate greeter?

Heather was very cordial and friendly, while she appeared to be playing a fast modified version of "Ten Questions." Without the slightest of hints or suggestions from me, she openly apologized as she admitted to trading out several pieces of furniture from my office several days prior to my arrival. Where I came from, such behavior is usually called pilfering! She mumbled something about the furniture in my office matched the décor of her office a little better, so she considered it her responsibility, and in the best interest for interior decorating, to initiate the trade. I later learned that *all* the furniture in my office was traded out, prior to my arrival, in *after hours* sessions by various other "corporate" managers throughout the building. What I thought at first was an intentional eclectic look for the décor of my office turned out to be a collection of items more appropriate for a White Elephant Sale.

That's enough about those first-day-on-the-job fantasies.

As I leaned back in my chair, realizing it probably gave new meaning to the game of executive musical chairs, I looked over my "To Do" list of priorities that needed to be completed over the next several days. The task of preparing for my first year performance review was circled, starred and thoughtfully positioned right at the top of the list. The paperwork for my performance review needed to be completed and submitted to my manager within the week. My manager and I were scheduled to meet in five days to discuss the progress I'd made over the past year. In addition, I needed to schedule and complete the annual performance reviews of all my direct reports within two weeks after *my* review. The sequence seemed rather unusual to me considering I've always met with my manager *after* meeting with each of my direct reports.

Rather than just sitting down and filling in boxes and checking off rating scales on the six page performance review sheet, better known as "corporate" form number PR-125644, I first preferred looking at the big picture. Summarizing the year in perspective and *then* organizing my thoughts for compliance with form PR-125644 seemed to make more sense, at least to me. The six pages of performance review forms were a little overwhelming. Did I really want to get started on it this late on a Friday afternoon?

Even though I was thinking about leaving for the day, the digital clock on my desk was only showing it to be 4:15 pm. I had a few more minutes to kill before I'd leave, which was usually around 4:30 pm. I say "kill" because over the years, I've come to realize my peak "mental" time is usually early morning to early afternoon. In the late afternoon my mind automatically shifts into "Park." Keep in mind that those of us in the "corporate" office don't punch a time card, but it felt like we did. Somehow I was subconsciously compelled to stay until at least 4:30 pm. Within two weeks after starting with the company, I quickly realized there was an unwritten policy about violating the informal, but sacred, 4:30 rule. The rule wasn't written anywhere on paper, but you sure knew it existed and was strictly adhered to. Should anyone decide or need to leave early for either business or personal reasons, one of the other "corporate" managers invariably appeared. There he would be, standing in the hall or in his doorway right on your path to the exit. You know the routine. In what he pretends to be a soft, low-toned casual voice, while looking at his watch, would say something like "It's getting about that time, huh!" Keep in mind, his soft, low-toned casual voice was more like the town crier using an amplified megaphone breaking the latest breaking news story for everyone to hear. The exaggerated look at his watch was quickly followed by a direct stare at the unsuspecting one, usually over the top of his glasses, as if his head was immobile and the rest of his face needed to keep looking down at his watch. After the six-word question and over-the-spectacles glance, he managed to survey up and down the hall to see if anyone else might have heard. For your information, I religiously get into the office by 6:30 am every day and rarely take a lunch break longer than forty-five minutes, most often right there at my desk. You know, new employees do things like that.

You ask yourself, "When does "corporate Carusso" usually get to the office?"

"Oh, generally around 8:01 am."

"How about *his* lunch break?"

"I'm not one to keep score, but let's just say he usually starts picking his teeth around 1:45 after returning from lunch."

In looking back over this past year, my mind gradually drifts back to the interview and hiring process I so graciously endured. Being an analytical type, I logically start at the beginning. Gosh, that seems so long ago! Several scenes and reruns stand out, remaining quite vivid in my mind. Things that, for whatever reasons, were permanently etched into my brain and will never be forgotten. Every minute detail, from the exact words that were uttered to the precise number of books neatly arranged on the shelf. My manager, who, by the way, is a "corporate" Vice President and constantly manages to remind and let everyone know his relative position in the pecking order, was quite accurate about the initial challenges I would face on the job. He never mentioned anything about the "corporate" office dynamics and politics that consumed the building.

One vivid pre-employment memory that came to mind had my manager and me discussing my compensation and the total employee benefits package. He went to great pains as he dramatically pulled the "corporate" manager's compensation sheet out of the policy and procedures manual. As a potential candidate for hire to the company, I didn't quite understand why he had it locked in the left-hand bottom drawer of his desk. I've always considered a policies and procedures manual a working document that should be kept confidential, but wasn't keeping it locked a little drastic? As he leaned over his chair arm to get the manual, I remember noticing his shiny desktop didn't have a single fingerprint mark or smudge on it. Even though he never let me actually look at or read the pages he was referring to in the policy and procedures manual, he continually pointed to and referenced them as if I could see the page(s). He went to great lengths to convince me that when "he" extends an employment offer, the accompanying compensation package "he" presents is always at the top end for that particular position's job classification. He also stressed that it was "his" policy, along with implying it was also company policy, to offer the best compensation and relocation package "he" could. Supposedly, he didn't want to play the compensation negotiating game and would always start out with "his best" offer.

After a person achieves or has been at the level of a "corporate" manager for a number of years, he is undoubtedly interested in maximizing his financial compensation and benefits package. However, research has proven that "money" is *not* the only motivator when a person considers a new position and relocation. The last time I read some of the research studies, financial considerations ranked around fifth or sixth on the list. Things like quality of work life, involvement in decision making, future opportunities, quality of personal life, location and proximity to amenities, and a host of other variables are usually factored into a potential new employee's decision matrix. In my case, salary wasn't even in my top ten list of primary motivating factors under consideration, and it must have been easy to tell. Why play the negotiating game if you're told by your potential future manager that "he" always makes the "best" offer and that he doesn't believe in negotiating?

I actually accepted the "corporate" position with a salary and compensation package substantially lower than what I had with my previous employer. However, my other motivating factors, which had nothing to do with the company or the job, more than made up for my immediate, or was that permanent, financial loss. Upon my formal acceptance of the position, and as we were casually talking in his office, my manager unnecessarily seemed to dwell on the fact that my salary and compensation package "would definitely surpass and exceed" my previous compensation "within a year or two."

Today, rumor around the office has it that all salary increases for the next two years will probably be frozen, as they have been for the past two years. Supposedly, it had something to do with a downturn in the entire industry. Now I wonder how old those pre-employment financials were that I read...

Someone startled me out of my daydreaming by slamming a door not too far from my office. Making sure my office was still undisturbed, I took another glance at my watch. It was only 4:18. Should I leave? Maybe not yet. Who knows who was serving as the hall monitor this afternoon. Glancing down the hall, just in case, I couldn't help but notice several heads quickly popping in and out of several office doorways, but, for some unknown reason, no bodies emerged attached to those heads. It looked like a carnival shooting gallery where the targets quickly appear and just as quickly disappear. Maybe the slamming door startled them too...

Pulling the middle drawer of my desk open, as if to be doing something important, I notice a recent memo dated last week that was distributed to all of us "corporate" manager types. The memo was a reminder from the company's VP of Transportation, letting us know that our company automobiles would no longer be part of our compensation packages effective the first of next month. The memo stated that it was simply a follow-up to what we were told via a previous memo, and verbally by our Vice Presidents, last year. In the memo from last year, which I got a copy of just last week, we were given the option of purchasing our company automobiles at what was considered a fair market value. Fair market value was determined by the VP of Transportation. No matter what the price was, somehow I couldn't envision myself willingly owning a Yugo. Okay, it really wasn't a Yugo! In a cost cutting move, the Board of Directors decided to eliminate all corporate autos as part of our compensation packages for *all* corporate managers. In place of the automobile, we were going to be paid what the board called a "substantial" monthly car allowance instead. After calculating deductions, taxes, and costs of insuring our own personal cars for business purposes, that Yugo is starting to look real good.

The board's decision was made last year, with the original memo sent three hundred ninety-seven days ago. Senility could possibly be setting in, or I could be experiencing a little dementia, but the elimination of the perk called a company automobile was never brought up three hundred seventy-two days ago. In fact, the automobile was specifically highlighted and factored into my compensation package when I received and subsequently accepted the offer. Being the practical person that I am (My wife says it's more a definition of being cheap instead of practical, especially when I'm able to squeeze the buffalo on a nickel so tight I can make it burp!), I sold my personal car shortly after starting my new job. Had I known about the pending policy change, my decision to sell would have been different.

Did I mention that we're going car shopping this weekend?

Just like the saying that a watched pot never boils, time seems to stand still when you watch the clock. Again I glanced at my watch and noticed that it was only 4:23 pm. Without even realizing I was doing it, I put the watch close to my ear to make sure it was still running. When you think about it, bringing the watch to my ear made absolutely no sense at all considering that it's one of those electronic watches and doesn't make any noise.

Okay, with about seven minutes to go, maybe I should make one final check of my voicemail. Checking your voicemail late on a Friday afternoon is like putting a period at the end of a well-written sentence. Somehow the action of making sure there are no new recent calls puts closure to the past five days and leaves a sense of having no unfinished business cluttering your mind over the weekend. But that feeling of closure vanished quickly when I looked again at my long "To Do" list sitting in front of me.

"You have two new messages. Would you like to review them?" blared the electronic voice over the phone. During my orientation to the intricacies of the phone system on my first day at the office, I had to make a very critical decision. I had the choice of either a *male* or *female* electronic voice about to lead me through the voicemail menus. Naturally, you can guess which one I chose. Responding to the electronic maiden on the other end of the line, I chose yes by punching the #1 button. The first message was the computerized voice of a vendor wanting to discuss a "professional" subscription to the *Workplace Safety and Compliance Newsletter.* You know what I did with that message... I get great satisfaction from pressing the #9 button. The electronic maiden's voice then informed me that message number one was deleted. Did you ever wonder where those messages, or electrons or whatever that message is made up of, go? The electronic lady then made a flawless segue into the second message.

"Hi, Bryan. This is Bruno from Break-All Moving Company. Well, we're still working on processing your damage claim from your move. We'll be needing three more receipts from those items you claimed were damaged by my movers. Give me a call at 880-4...." He said the numbers so fast, followed by what might have been the word "thanks," that I couldn't understand anything after the number four. Seems funny that he even gave me his number, considering that I've been calling

Personal Values

him weekly for the past year. Somehow our relationship is based on what's becoming a futile attempt on my part to resolve a simple damage claim. I'm becoming convinced that Bruno attended one of those special customer service seminars that teaches participants simple techniques on how to drag out a customer complaint long enough so the customer finally just gives up! I, too, can play that game! So my tactic is to wait until Monday to return his call. It's only my loss that's being drug out. I pressed the #7 button and the electronic maiden dutifully told me that message number two would be archived. She then asked if I would like to do anything else. Seems like a dumb question, doesn't it? I've learned to listen and respond to all of her instructions, because if we don't, she gets her revenge. She develops a "secret" report at the end of each month stating who, and how many times we didn't fully adhere to "Telephone Policy." Is "Big Brother" watching?

Bruno's message made my mind drift back in time and rerun a conversation I had with my VP weeks before accepting this position. As we were discussing the company's relocation package and the interstate movement of household goods to our new home, he reassured me several times about the generous and "unparalleled" relocation package available for those of us with "corporate" manager rank and status. Under the circumstances at the time, I decided not to inquire into the particulars of the relocation policy. Such a reputable company surely had a decent relo package. Again, he was clutching, with knuckles turning white, the policies and procedures manual, and emphatically stated that "No one has *ever* lost financially in making a relocation for this company. In fact, many people have actually come out ahead from the generous and lucrative relocation package." That was good enough for me.

When all was said and done after the move, except for the small problem with Bruno, my tax accountant calculated that the move personally set me back just under ten thousand dollars *after* all reimbursements from the company. With documents in hand and adhering to all appropriate company procedures and protocol, I sat down with my VP to discuss my accountant's calculations. By now I had my own copy of the policies and procedures manual to refer to, which I was told to keep locked up and never share with my staff. My VP was very good at dispensing sympathy, notice that I didn't say empathy, along with being well-versed and rehearsed at saying, "Well, I just don't understand it. We've never had this happen before. Unfortunately, there is nothing I, or the company, can do now to help you out." As he said this, he simultaneously raised his hand toward his mouth and chin, as if in a thoughtful mode, helping to disguise the obvious tension in his voice. Come to think about it, during that whole conversation he never once had direct eye contact with me.

The ten thousand dollar loss is something I prefer forgetting about, so without realizing it, I was holding my briefcase and walking out my office door. Another involuntary quick glance at my watch indicated it was 4:29 pm. Briskly walking toward the door, I couldn't help but notice the desk tops in every office along the way were perfectly clean, everything in neat stacks and in perfect order. Quickly glancing into most of the offices along my route, I noticed a number of the other "corporate" managers conspicuously staring at their watches as I walked by.

I was now thirty feet from the employee entrance. Will I make it this time?

No! Not a chance! Just as I got to the exit door, I heard from behind me a deep resonating masculine voice. I'll swear the voice was amplified well above the one hundred forty decibel level. Echoing throughout the hallway came the question, "Bryan, I see it's getting about that time, huh?"

Personal Values

I replied with a semi cheerful, "Sure is. Have a nice weekend!"

Chapter II

Some Call It the Way They Want It...

> *Dare to be true: nothing can need a lie;*
> *A fault, which needs it most, grows two thereby.*
> *Herbert 1593-1633*

One of the first significant tests or rites of passage of becoming a "man" happens when a boy goes out for the first time to play organized little league baseball. Today, people call it "organized" little league baseball. Believe me, it was, and still is, anything *but* organized. Have you ever seen five-, six-, and seven-year-olds organized? And then there are the parents... but that's another story about maturity and role modeling behavior.

Having been born in the first year of what's now considered the "baby boomer" generation, we didn't play "tee" ball like some "organized" groups do today. That's not to say we shouldn't have, though. When batting, we came up to the plate to face another *little* leaguer who was usually the biggest kid in the community, but still qualified age-wise to play little league. Instead of baseball, the *big* pitchers should have been going out

Personal Values

for Sumo wrestling. Talk about their pitching accuracy, there was none. Most of the time when it was your turn to go to the plate, it seemed more like target practice, but unfortunately, you, the batter, were the target. At that age, it's hard to explain to a five-year-old the concept of a strike zone, especially when you're positioned in the batter's box and see a projectile approaching in your general direction at what seems like three hundred miles per hour.

One Saturday morning during practice, our coach scheduled a *real live* little league umpire to be an inspirational guest speaker at our weekly "dugout discussion session." Our dugout sessions were where we supposedly discussed and learned the finer points and techniques of baseball. Even though our guest speaker was a retired truck driver, he was still our official umpire and commanded our complete respect and admiration. His presentation was going to focus on the complex subject of the "strike zone." When Mr. Rudy arrived at the ballpark, we were all in awe. What a significant emotional event for a kid to have a real live, official, little-league umpire actually visiting with us in the flesh. During the discussion, Walter, our third baseman, asked Mr. Rudy how he knows when to call the pitch a ball or strike. The rest of us thought it was a very insightful and well thought out question. Mr. Rudy went into a long philosophical dissertation, which we all listened to very intently but probably didn't really grasp or understand. His finger and stick drawings on the dirt were a little difficult to interpret. Near the end of what most of us thought was oratory genius, Mr. Rudy finally summarized the discussion by saying he has three choices when he observes the ball coming into the general proximity of home plate. One, he can "call it as it is." Two, he can "call it as he sees it." Or three, he can "call it as he thinks it should be." What pearls of wisdom for a little leaguer! His visit and words of inspiration during our "dugout discussion" would remain etched in all our minds forever. Unfortunately, his efforts didn't help our batting averages or strike out records very much.

Interestingly enough, and we didn't know it at that time, the wisdom and lessons from Mr. Rudy seem to have greater practical application today in the world of American "corporate" management than organized little league baseball. Thank you Mr. Rudy!

Wilma Kelly recently completed her Master's degree and joined the company immediately after graduation. Wilma is a little rough around the edges and doesn't seem very comfortable working in team or group situations. One might easily infer that she was "socially awkward," nothing time and experience couldn't fix. On the other hand, she was quite astute, very focused, analyzed situations very well for her age, and had exceptional project management skills. She was hired by the company to do a comprehensive needs analysis, then design and implement a new training program for the telephone sales department. If successful, she would then address the training and development needs of the customer service group. Both tasks would be quite formidable. Without ever having supervised anyone in the past, Wilma inherited a direct report by the name of Stephen Jordan. Stephen was very energetic and required high maintenance, meaning he needed constant supervision and direction to keep him focused on the task at hand. If anyone could possibly do that, it was probably Wilma. Over time, Wilma and Stephen seemed to balance each other quite well. Wilma had the know-how, and Stephen had the ability to implement, work with, and associate extremely well with others. Stephen, following the career path of many trainers we've seen in other companies across the United States, was involuntarily delegated to a trainer's role because the organization didn't know what else to do with him. His experience consisted of approximately eight years on the production floor, during which he kept requesting a reassignment. He may not have had the formal education, training, and experience to be an effective trainer, but his heart and desires were sure there. In looking at his situation from a bigger picture, I guess Stephen represents a breath of fresh air. Most companies make trainers out of individuals who are a few years from retirement and are only interested in counting the number of days till their sixty-fifth birthday, regardless of qualifications.

Around four o'clock one afternoon, as I was finishing a report for presentation the next morning at a department meeting, Wilma came into my office and lightly knocked on the open door. As I looked up from my monitor, I couldn't help but notice that she seemed distressed. The look on her face, the concentration in her eyes, along with her overall body language said, "I need someone to talk to, NOW!"

Being astute and quick to pick up on these kinds of verbal and non-verbal cues, I invited Wilma into my office and offered her a chair. As she readily accepted my offer and started to move in from the door, she turned around and gently closed the door, making sure it latched shut. This was one of those times I wasn't sure if I should stay on my side of the desk, or venture around to the other side, as I usually do, when I visit with people in my office. It's a subliminal thing on my part, about having physical barriers between me and the person I'm talking with. Quickly recognizing that she didn't appear to be ballistic and wasn't staring directly into my eyes, I surmised her distress wasn't directed towards me. I concluded this meeting in all likelihood would not be confrontational. The need for a physical barrier between us appeared to be minimal, so I made my way around to the other side of my desk and sat in another chair partially angled toward the front and side of Wilma.

Some Call It the Way They Want It...

I didn't have to search for any words to start the conversation; Wilma took care of that. Seems a lot of people seek me out when they find themselves in a dilemma or needing a sounding board. Maybe I should hang a shingle on my door, or under my plastic nameplate, and start charging by the hour! Another profit center in my department might not be a bad idea. Maybe it's the empathetic look on my face, or maybe the way I carry myself, but this type of thing happens to me no matter where I am. My wife and I can be grocery shopping, and as we're casually walking down the canned goods aisle it'll happen. Some cute little old lady will pick me out of all the others in the aisle, stop me, then proceed to ask me questions about a particular product she's contemplating purchasing. It's especially embarrassing trying to explain to my wife afterwards that I didn't know this little old lady... In another instance, we were walking together in a strange city on vacation when out of the hundreds of others in close proximity to us, a stranger made eye contact with me, approached me and proceeded to ask for directions. Why not pick on any of the other hundreds of people who probably look like they know where they're going? Not two tourists!

I probably should take Wilma's visit as a compliment. My secretary told me one day that throughout the "corporate" office, I've developed a reputation for helping others, empathizing, and being able to listen well. My secretary should know, seems she knows *everything* that goes on in the entire office complex, sometimes even before it happens. I still don't know how she does it.

"I must be losing my mind," Wilma started. I could quickly tell I didn't need to say anything for Wilma to keep talking. All I needed to do was partially raise my eyebrows and have that puzzled look on my face. Sure enough, Wilma picked up on it. "I don't know exactly where to begin," she said, "but here goes." I had no idea where this conversation was going to go,

Personal Values

or for how long, but it was obvious that Wilma sure needed someone to talk to.

I can't remember her exact words or the chronological sequence of her story, because she jumped all over the place as she was explaining it to me, but it went something like this:

Wilma was originally hired into the company as an Educational Specialist within the telephone sales department. Now, what exactly is an Educational Specialist? I surmised that they gave her that nebulous title to make her feel like a critical player, and possibly to make her *feel* important. As with most "specialist" positions within the company, she had limited responsibility and absolutely no authority. Other than supervise Stephen, she had absolutely no other "management" functions to perform. Considering her short tenure with the company, she said she really enjoyed her working relationships with all the telephone sales personnel and especially her manager, Esther. From all outward appearances, they got along very well and seemed to have established well-defined goals and objectives for Wilma's role. Word around the office was that Wilma was making great strides and establishing a reputation for being an innovator, while Stephen did most of the "grunt" work. To the surprise of Wilma, Esther, and most of the "corporate" office, the "powers that be" decided to do a little corporate reorganizing. Someone on the executive team must have recently read a condensed version of one of those "re-engineering" books that were so popular several years ago. Now that I reflect back on what Wilma told me, it was probably one of those condensed talking books on tape instead. How many in the "powers that be" group do you think actually read books? They usually spend more time on a daily basis nervously scanning their stock portfolio on the Internet than transacting legitimate company business. As a result of the unannounced reorganization, Wilma was now going to report through a newly created division that would provide "training and development" support services to the entire corporation. She would no longer be reporting through Esther in the telephone sales department. Sounded a little like the age-old battle of corporate centralization versus de-centralization.

Oh well, what's in a reporting relationship anyway? The important thing for Wilma was moving ahead with the goals and objectives she and Esther established for the telephone sales personnel. Wilma was still going to be responsible for that project. At the time of the reorganization, Wilma and Stephen were designing and developing a number of training classes that were the direct result of the extensive needs assessment she had previously conducted. Managers within the telephone sales functions were delighted with her performance and long-term direction and, for the first time in recent company history, were constantly requesting her services. She was a breath of fresh air compared to all the previous trainers the company had. The telephone sales department managers were very impressed with the results they were now starting to achieve with Wilma's help.

It was about two months after the low-keyed informal announcement about the reorganization that Wilma had her first face-to-face meeting with her new VP. In fact, she never heard from him, either by phone, FAX, or e-mail, until one day when her phone rang. The voice on the other end of the line said in a blunt but formal manner: "Wilma, this is Dave Rogers. I'm going to be visiting the corporate office for the next two days. I have a few people to visit with, and I was hoping you and I could get together for an hour or so. I'm traveling today, so how would tomorrow morning about eight o'clock be for you?" Dave Rogers didn't work at the corporate office, instead, he worked out of his home in another part of the country.

Dave showed up at exactly eight o'clock the next morning and proceeded to ask Wilma a series of questions about her goals and objectives, including all the commitments she'd scheduled for the next six months or so. Her schedule was heavily booked and getting worse by the day because of all the requests from the telephone sales department managers. Dave listened, then asked a number of what he probably considered to be probing questions. Without ever commenting on anything that Wilma said, Dave continued asking questions and making notes in a small portfolio he kept out of Wilma's view. She thought to herself that his behavior was representative of the way some VPs *think* they should act, something to do with the "information is power" myth. For Wilma, "*shared* information was power." I hope she still has that same attitude when and if she ever moves into a "corporate" manager's role.

After about forty-five minutes of one-way conversation, with Wilma responding to a barrage of questions, and Dave scribbling notes, he looked at his watch and said he needed to get to a nine o'clock appointment scheduled with another one of the VPs. Wilma said Dave made an effort to highlight "VP," almost as if to imply that he had more important people to meet with instead of talking with her.

"You know, Wilma, I have to schedule my time very tightly when I come here to the "corporate" office so I can complete everything I need to do in the short time I'm here," Dave said. "Wilma, what you're doing sounds rather interesting, but I'd like you to fulfill *only* the commitments you've made for the next six months or so and not commit to any others. What I want you to do is develop a proposal for a comprehensive sales training program that would include and focus on the entire sales force, not just telephone sales. Next month when I'm in town again, I would like to schedule an appointment with the President, and several other VPs to review your proposal and gain approval for funding and implementation of a comprehensive, self-paced, computer assisted sales training program. I'll let you know the dates I'll be here next month. I usually like to get out here around the third week of each month. Oh, and I almost forgot, give me a copy of your daily schedule for the next six months."

Without a "good bye," "thank you," or any other type of closure, Dave quickly folded his notebook, which is known by others as his trademark, and proceeded out the door.

"You talk about hitting me with a wet towel," Wilma said to me. "Over the last two months, he never called or as much as sent me an e-mail to say hello, and now today he's telling me to stop what I'm doing and go in another direction. During that two month period, I left him several e-mails, voicemail messages, and even several faxes asking to get together so we could at least meet, but he never even had the courtesy to respond to any of them," Wilma said very disgustedly. According to Wilma, the direction Dave seems to want to go is wrought with problems, and according to her, doomed for certain failure.

Well, enough of the details about their initial meeting. Wilma diligently worked for the next four weeks, between commitments, on Dave's requested proposal. The most difficult part for her was saying "no" to requests for additional help and training by the managers in the telephone sales function. She found it difficult to tell the requesting managers that her VP didn't want her committing her time to them, even if it was for services they deemed necessary, very important, and contributed to their department's bottom line.

The meeting the following month included Dave Rogers, the President, the Executive Vice President, Stephen, and Wilma. Wilma could recall and describe every last detail about the meeting, or at least as she talked, it seemed that way. Needless to say, she *did* describe everything to me. What she found most revealing during the meeting was how uncomfortable and nervous Dave Rogers seemed to be while in the company of the President and Executive VP. During the meeting, Wilma presented the proposal and did most of the talking. Periodically Dave would try to make a point for what he thought was a clarification or would direct a question at Wilma, but most of his comments seemed inappropriate or were intentionally ignored by the rest of the participants. He must have felt out of place and totally out of control. As you might guess, Wilma had written the entire proposal, so it was slanted to her philosophy and way of thinking. She had presented a very comprehensive proposal for the sales training program including its structure and proposed implementation steps. The President and Executive Vice President made a few suggestions and constructive comments, but overall, they were in complete agreement and full support of her proposal. Their nod of approval and request to get it moving immediately was all Wilma needed to hear. Stephen, probably because of his immaturity, is overwhelmed and intimidated by anyone he thinks holds a "power" position. He had only four words to say during the hour and a half meeting: "Good morning" as he shook hands with everyone, and "Thank you!" as they all left the President's office. The only one leaving the office with a frown was Dave.

Wilma felt very pumped up after the meeting. Well, why not! Instead of working on a training program focused only toward the telephone sales department personnel, she was now getting the "executive" nod to move ahead on a project that would potentially impact *all* the corporate-wide sales functions. Now she could go back to some of those managers who requested her services, the ones she had had to turn down for the previous month. Now she could let them know they would be beneficiaries of an even better program focused on training their sales people. Even though she was skeptical of where

Dave was headed during their initial meeting the previous month, Wilma now surmised he probably had been envisioning the sales training and development functions from a bigger and more centralized perspective. She was now asking herself why she had been so myopic in her view at that time?

Wilma is one of those compulsive personality types and likes to write up minutes or summaries after every meeting she attends or participates in. She said her memory wasn't always the best after a week or two, so in writing a meeting summary, she could avoid the possible future embarrassment of forgetting or overlooking any important details discussed in that meeting. The meeting with the President was definitely one she was going to write a summary for. Because of the importance of the meeting, she wanted to commit to paper the major points, conclusions, and agreements reached. Even though she was usually compulsive about writing minutes after every meeting, this one was especially critical to do so. To progress in a timely manner, a number of the conclusions and subsequent steps in completing the project would require substantial resources, both financial and personnel. As a matter of record, the minutes would summarize and clarify the conclusions and agreements made. Future confusion or misunderstandings would be eliminated, or at least minimized. Wilma's habit of writing minutes is a practice I and many others should get in the habit of doing more often.

Before forwarding the final version of her minutes to everyone at the meeting, Wilma considered it a professional courtesy to send a copy to Dave Rogers for his review. Dave might be able to provide additional insights she might have omitted before forwarding copies to the President, Executive Vice President, and Stephen. She also thought of it as a goodwill gesture to proactively take steps to develop her working relationship with Dave. She was practicing that old "What can I do to help this situation" philosophy. On the other hand, Wilma thought,

Dave would be actively involved and/or could be influential in making this project a company-wide success. As one of the VPs reporting to the Executive Vice President, Dave could be influential in "bird dogging" any unforeseen problems.

Wilma e-mailed the minutes to Dave Rogers and requested his feedback. What she was actually doing was looking for his limited blessing. What she got back from Dave was more than a surprise! As she was conveying this part of the story, she pulled out a five-page document from the notebook she had laying on the floor next to my desk. And in a voice I'm certain was heard five offices away, she literally shouted, "Look at this!" Unfortunately I'm not an Evelyn Wood Reading Dynamics graduate, so reading the five pages took more time than a cursory glance at the top page. E-mail technology is fascinating, and at times, a time-saver. Fortunately, because of the technology, I didn't have to read *two* documents, the one Wilma wrote and then the one Dave rewrote. Dave demonstrated his marginal Microsoft Word expertise by inserting in bold what he wanted said in the document while italicizing the parts of Wilma's text he wanted changed or eliminated. Most of the document was in italics. I was beginning to wonder if Wilma and Dave were recalling and writing about the same meeting! Wilma's version was to *day*, as Dave's version was to *night*! According to Wilma, Dave was surely in the *dark*.

As I mentioned earlier, Wilma is a little rough around the edges, but like a pit bulldog with a short fuse, you instinctively sense the need to keep on her good side. She indicated that when she received Dave's response, she started to question her own sanity and ability to recall what happened during what she called the "President's Meeting." She also assured me there was no history of amnesia in her family tree.

Remember earlier when I mentioned she had good project management and analytical skills? Well, she composed herself and gave a copy of Dave's response to Stephen, asking for his reaction to Dave's input. She told me Stephen was completely shocked by what he read, stating he didn't remember the events and conclusions as Dave did. Wilma also said Stephen hedged a lot and reserved his personal views while trying to rationalize some of Dave's comments.

Okay, now she knew she wasn't experiencing any form of dementia, as least from Stephen's perspective. So what should she do now? Based on her strong personal convictions, that question was easy for Wilma to answer. There were only two others in the "President's Meeting" besides Stephen and Dave, the President and the Executive Vice President. Why not get more input, at least from one of them? That's the sign of a real analytical mind. Here comes the bulldog again!

Wilma said she casually bumped into the Executive Vice President the following day. She never did say what she meant by "casually." I suspect it was more like calculated and intentional. By choice, she waited until the following day so she could, as she said, cool down. How and where the "casually" took place, she didn't offer, nor did I ask. Wilma supposedly shared just one portion of the five-page document with the Executive Vice President, who, to her sense of relief and personal sanity, told her what the President said (at the "President's Meeting") and what was written in bold print on the page were diametrically opposed. "The President *never* would say something like that!" the Executive Vice President told Wilma. The entire section that the Executive Vice President read was in bold print.

Wilma felt a wonderful sense of relief. She was now convinced she wasn't experiencing any type of mental lapse or "senior moment." She could delay, at least for a few more years,

Personal Values

completing that AARP application. Now, with ammunition in hand, what she felt she had to do was call Dave and discuss his "bold" comments.

Finally, the reason for our conversation today was at hand. Her call with Dave didn't go very well, at least from Wilma's point of view. Sometimes there can be a great void between what a person says and how he says it, but I can only imagine the intensity of their phone conversation. Oh, to have been a "bug" on the line during that call...

The bottom line – my conversation with Wilma happened because, in the end, Dave "directed," or did she say he "ordered" her, to send the minutes out to each of the participants, eliminating the italics and including only the "bold" print without any editing. Period!

Now it's 6:30 pm and I'm lost for words. What do you say or what kind of advice do you give Wilma? It's also getting late, and after almost two and a half hours of sitting and intently listening to her, I'm getting tired.

What popped into my mind but the wisdom of Mr. Rudy! Yes! That's it!

"Wilma," I said, "some *call it as it is*, while others *call it as they want it!*"

Chapter III

Do As I Say, Not As I Do

> *Those he commands move only in command,*
> *Nothing in love, now does he feel his title*
> *Hang loose about him, like a giant's robe*
> *Upon a dwarfish thief.*
>
> *Shakespeare 1564-1616*

One of my earlier lives, better known as one of the first jobs I had in the "real" business world, and after leaving the ivory tower of undergraduate and graduate academics, was that of Employment Manager for a large subsidiary of a Fortune 100 company. The decade was an interesting and dynamic time to observe and participate in some major social changes occurring in the United States, as well as the rest of the world. It was a time not only to observe, but also to be part of many historical social changes as they were occurring and affecting the direction and evolution of the world of work. I'm talking about the early to mid 70s. No, I'm not talking about my age, but the 1970s: Vietnam; the various minority and women's movement(s); federal, state, and local laws challenging and impacting all aspects of employment practices; civil rights;

Personal Values

counter cultures; alternative lifestyles; personal expression and individuality in clothes, grooming, music, and the list goes on and on.

One of the areas of responsibility I had as Employment Manager included college relations and national recruitment. Even though my staff did most of the job fairs, career days, and college interviewing, I found great satisfaction in visiting various colleges and universities around the country to assist my staff, in addition to interviewing college seniors during our "crunch" periods. There's a feeling of excitement and vibrancy on college campuses during the annual recruiting and interviewing months. That excitement is unparalleled in the business world, at least from what I've experienced. The closest I've come to it is planting and harvest time in the American Midwest. In thinking back on those recruiting and interviewing days, which should have been spelled "daze" instead of "days," I'm reminded of a television commercial that aired in the late 70s. The commercial depicted what appeared to be several elementary school students attempting what most of us would consider an impossible feat. Following the visual, the commentator for the commercial stated "they (the students) keep trying because they don't know they can't do it." Seniors in college, anticipating graduation, seem to possess that same type of "can do" mentality. From their perspective, there is nothing in the world of work they can't do.

Back then, as inexperienced recruiters and interviewers, one of the questions we generally asked potential candidates was what their long-term career goals and objectives were. Long-term to us meant five to ten years. Without having scientific evidence or research studies to back up my following statement, I suggest you use yourself as a scientific sample of one. A majority of students would respond with something like this, "I would like to gain a little hands-on experience and then eventually move into *management*."

Bradley Erickson was one such person who probably said just that when he was interviewed by the company recruiter. When he joined the company approximately eleven years ago fresh out of college, he knew he wanted to be in field sales and then eventually move into sales "*management*." Bradley was one of those individuals who would never take "no" for an answer. He didn't know what the word "no" meant. His sales performance for the first eight years was good. He always made his sales numbers, and seemed to have good rapport with all his customers. Rumor had it that some of his sales tactics were a little questionable at times. Notice I said "tactics." Bradley was a "tactical" seller, one who could successfully compete at the same level and in the same category as the winner of last year's New York City "Used Car Salesman of the Year" competition. His sales strategy and strategic planning skills had a lot to be desired, and that's stating it mildly.

With the growth of the company during his first eight years as a Territory Sales Representative, several vacancies occurred in the Regional Sales Manager ranks. After eight years, Bradley was finally selected, if not by default then by his tenure, to fill one of them. After having applied for every sales manager vacancy over a five-year period, he demonstrated time and again his resilience from rejection. I'm not sure if his final selection was based on his perceived potential as a sales manager or the fact that everyone knew his name and they eventually felt sorry for him. In his case, persistence paid off. None the less, for the last three years of his career with the company, he's proudly distributed his business card showing the title of "Regional Sales Manager" under his name. His dream came true; he was now in *management* with a total of eight regional sales representatives reporting directly to him.

Personal Values

As sales manager, Bradley would schedule quarterly sales meetings with all of his sales team. He felt quarterly sales meetings provided an opportunity for the salesmen under his charge to communicate, plan, train, share war stories, and relax. He said it was "sort of a two-day sales R&R for his men!" Bradley liked to use military analogies like calling the competition "enemies," or referring to customers' offices as the "front line." Even though he never served in any branch of the armed forces, he could go on for hours comparing sales to military tactics.

I was approached by Bradley and asked to attend, and participate, at his third quarter sales meeting. He requested I fill the role of guest speaker and bring his team up to date on what was happening within my department. I always welcomed these types of in-house speaking opportunities. Just attending the meeting was a great way to promote my department and develop the necessary business and customer service interfaces with sales. Did I mention that his quarterly sales meetings were generally held at "nice" resorts or conference centers in locations most of us would consider vacation destinations? Las Vegas, here we come!

For whatever reason, I arrived at the airport about an hour before the scheduled nonstop flight to Las Vegas. Without openly admitting it, I probably did plan it that way. Not that I'm a glutton for the intentional punishment commercial airlines and public airports seem to inflict on their customers, but I cherish the "quiet" or "down" time airline travel provides. Yes, "down" time! It's a great opportunity to shut out everything going on around me and try to catch up on my personal reading. On this particular trip, I decided to take two *National Geographic* magazines, one *Business Week*, and two *Time* magazines. And if that weren't enough, I carried, just in case, one of the books on the most recent *Business Week* top-ten best seller list. After traveling both domestically and internationally for the last twenty-five plus years, I've fine-tuned a sixth sense. I can blot out almost all of what's going on around me, but still maintain a level of environmental consciousness that picks up on any unique or unusual opportunity for "people watching." Notice I said unique or unusual. After two and a half decades of business traveling, I've seen and experienced just about everything a road warrior can experience, from emergency landings to having a ringside seat for several domestic disputes, at least three of which I'm convinced were eventually resolved in divorce court. My sixth sense radar capabilities can screen out the usual and ordinary, but throw up a red flag when "unique" or "unusual" is about to occur.

I was comfortably sitting at the departure gate and almost fully engrossed in an article on Egyptian Archeology (guess what magazine that is), when my sixth sense radar picked up a blip on its auditory screen. My sixth sense radar system also has a visual screen. Sure enough, I heard my name being called out. "Bryan! Bryan Matthews! I didn't know you were on this flight!" It was Bradley's voice. As I looked in the direction of his voice, I observed Bradley stepping over a few carry-on bags carelessly placed in the middle of the aisle of the passenger waiting area. The carry-on bags collectively served as a makeshift obstacle course for anyone attempting to navigate his way down the aisle. After analyzing the positioning of the bags, which were right in front of the feet of their owners, I suspected there were many "unseasoned" travelers waiting to get on our flight. Las Vegas is a vacation destination... With Bradley quickly approaching, I realized ancient tomb hieroglyphics would have to wait.

Bradley had just landed and was making this connection as the final leg on his trip to Las Vegas. I moved my strategically positioned briefcase from the chair next to where I was sitting. I do that to maintain my personal space and keep unwanted strangers from sitting too close. Bradley shook my hand and sat down. He was a little out of breath as he positioned his briefcase next to his feet. Before we had a chance to go through the usual getting reacquainted rituals and dialogue, Bradley said he was glad we had this chance to get together and "...talk *privately* before the meeting." When he said the word "privately," several heads turned our way and I'm sure their auditory scanners were tuned in for possible reception.

Annual performance reviews in the company have traditionally been scheduled during the fourth quarter of the calendar year. This year would be the third time Bradley would be doing them with each of his eight sales team members. This was one administrative and management task Bradley seemed to have difficulties with. Bradley said he felt such "administrivia" got in the way of his, and his team's, selling efforts. He indicated that even though all his salesmen were meeting, and in some cases, far exceeding their sales goals and objectives, they never seemed to achieve many of his "non-sales related expectations." According to Bradley his non-sales related expectations included many of the peripheral things like etiquette, grooming, and vocabulary, which contribute to the customers' image of a well-rounded sales professional. He asked if I would be so kind as to observe and make a few notes about all eight members of his sales team over the next couple days. He wanted me to especially focus my attention on what he called their "non-sales" skills and attributes. Afterwards, he wanted to get together to receive feedback on my thoughts and observations. Still a little unsure of what he precisely meant by "non-sales" I again asked him exactly what kinds of things he thought I should be looking for. His response was rather vague as he replied, "You know Bryan, all those things that make a salesman outstanding, head and shoulders above the competition. True Professionals!"

My exit-row window seat provided the legroom I needed to be reasonably comfortable, and fortunately on this trip, no one was assigned to the middle seat. Bradley was about six rows behind me, so I managed to immerse myself again in the Egyptian article, and the rest of the magazine, without interruption.

The strip in Las Vegas is an experience in sensory overload for anyone, whether it's a first or repeat visit. What a combination: Las Vegas and one of our company's sales teams. Seems most of our company salesmen live by the philosophy of "work hard, play hard," and such was the case for Bradley and his sales team. The days were scheduled with nonstop meetings, with a little recreation squeezed in on the last day. Group dinners occupied the evenings. What happened after dinner? I'm not sure I really want to know, but I could sure guess, after hearing some of the innuendoes and inside jokes each morning before, and during, the sessions. Loud noises were less than welcome each morning while the volume of non-alcoholic fluids consumed during the meetings increased daily... Doesn't alcohol contribute to dehydration?

For me, three days and nights in Las Vegas was more than enough. Traveling as much as I have over my career, I find motel rooms, airports, restaurants, and even towns all start to look the same. About five years ago when I recapped that year's accomplishments (it was with a different company), I counted two hundred twenty-one nights on the road and away from home. That's entirely too much!

Observing Bradley's sales team was like standing in the audio and television departments of an electronics store on a Sunday afternoon and attempting to watch simultaneous football games on multiple television sets. Well, maybe not quite that bad, but it was equivalent to watching a three-ring circus with great acts being performed at the same time in all three rings.

Personal Values

Periodically throughout the three-day meeting, Bradley would *privately* ask if I noticed anything yet. If he anticipated the potential was there for something to happen, he would try to inconspicuously alert me to be alert and ready. He wasn't very subtle in his approach, and I'm sure every one of the sales reps knew he was trying to *secretly* communicate something to me. His persistence finally convinced me he was serious about wanting feedback on my observations.

Before shaking hands and performing the standard rituals of separation with everyone on the last day of meeting, Bradley pulled me aside and said he was scheduled to be at the corporate office the following week. He asked, "Bryan, could you set some time aside next week for us to get together?"

"Sure Bradley. In fact, let's plan to have dinner one evening, that way we can take all the time we need and won't feel pressured by any other appointments or commitments during the day. How's this coming Thursday evening sound?" I asked.

"Great!" he replied. "I'll stop by your office sometime during the day to set a time and confirm."

From the time we left my office on Thursday afternoon and got seated at the restaurant, it couldn't have been more than thirty minutes. During those thirty minutes he reminded me of a three-year-old kid anxious for Christmas morning and the opportunity to tear into all the presents. Oh, those agonizing moments! Somehow though, I didn't feel I would be filling the Santa Claus role Bradley might be expecting.

"Well, Bryan, what did you observe about my people at the meeting last week in Las Vegas, and what do you think they need to do to improve?" Bradley asked. Even before the waitress had a chance to take two steps away from the table with our orders, he was leaning over the table on both elbows, anxiously awaiting my response.

"Bradley," I started in a soft voice, "you just asked me two questions in one, and from my perspective, both were the wrong questions to ask." As his face full of anticipation quickly changed to one of puzzlement, I continued, "Maybe your questions should have been first, *What did you observe in me last week?* and second, *What do I need to do to improve?*" Here's the story as I conveyed it to Bradley:

It's very difficult to provide constructive feedback to anyone without giving specific examples. In Bradley's case, very specific behaviors and actions would be more informative than generalities, whether it was about the group collectively, or individually. What Bradley originally asked me to do was to provide feedback on the behaviors and performance of others, his sales men, exclusive of him. I suspect Bradley was hoping I would provide him with insights and the magical "silver bullet" to correct or improve the performance of his subordinates. However, from my observations during the Las Vegas meeting, it was he, Bradley, who already possessed that "silver bullet." He just wasn't putting it to use.

During the three-day meeting in Las Vegas, I observed each salesman and made copious notes on what I saw. I also jotted down notes about Bradley, his actions, behaviors, and the role modeling he seemed to be demonstrating. We began by talking about the notes I'd made on him. The exact unedited list I gave him follows:

> Bradley - Day I – Arrival – Late afternoon – Unscheduled evening:
> - Spinning tires on rental auto in motel parking lot with salesmen as passengers in the vehicle

Personal Values

- Purchased six $160 bottles of wine with dinner along with several other rounds of drinks
- After numerous drinks, became loud, domineering, and used profanity
- Told off-color jokes while smoking cigars at the table – there was a mixed crowd at the semi-formal restaurant

Bradley - Day II – Daytime meetings – Evening group dinner:
- Started the meeting twenty-three minutes late
- Meeting drifted – agenda not followed
- Cutting salesmen short when they were talking – Told one salesman that he should have already known the answer to the question he was posing to the group
- Excessive flirting and carrying on with the waitress serving the evening dinner
- Implying that two salesmen were "wimps" (in front of the rest of the group) because they didn't care to go bar-hopping after dinner

Bradley - Day III – Morning meeting – Afternoon recreation – Evening dinner:
- Showed signs of being very tired and disorganized (maybe too much to drink the night before coupled with too little sleep)
- Started meeting nineteen minutes late
- Skipped agenda items just to get finished by "tee time" – some issues were left unresolved and on the table
- No closure or summary to the meeting
- Seemed to intimidate or force golf partners (and another foursome) into several wagers
- Violated golf course etiquette - drove golf cart rather recklessly – didn't adhere to ninety degree rule

- Some of the golf awards appeared inappropriate for salesmen to take home and show to the family
- Suggesting and organizing a group to go to a strip club after dinner

Bradley - Day IV – Departure – On your own:
- Didn't see Bradley

As he stared at the piece of paper with my notes about him, I could see the color draining from his face, his lips tightening, tension building throughout his whole body, and his hands starting to shake just a little. He was obviously expecting observations about his sales reps, not about him. Did I turn the heat up too much? Did I hit a nerve? How was he now going to respond? No, I couldn't back down now. Anyway, how could I? He had a copy of my notes right in front of him. I thought to myself, "Stay calm Bradley! We'll eventually get around to talking about your sales reps. Maybe then you'll refocus your attention away from yourself and onto your salesmen."

Before giving Bradley an opportunity to say a word, I tried to assure him I wasn't making any value judgments about him or his behavior at the meeting in Las Vegas. I was just trying to describe and explain to him what I observed about *his* actions and behaviors. Again, for a second time, I reminded him I'd share with him my observations of each of his salesmen. But first I wanted to demonstrate how his behaviors, at least from my point of view, influenced the behaviors of the rest of his team. I handed him a copy of a research study, from the *Harvard Business Review,* entitled "Influences on Employee Behavior." I explained that the study focused on the decisions and behaviors of subordinates and what motivating factors had the greatest influence on making their decisions and exhibiting certain behaviors. The number one influence was "The Behavior of One's Superior in the Company," followed by such things as "Ethical Climate of the Industry," and "Formal Company Policy – or Lack Thereof." He could read the whole article later if he wanted to.

I stopped talking while Bradley remained silent, intently staring at my observation notes. I was starting to get a little uncomfortable, still not knowing how he would react. He looked across the table at me, focusing directly into my eyes, and still didn't say a word for what seemed like an hour (in reality, it was probably less than fifteen seconds). Thank goodness, our food arrived! Somehow, I wasn't as hungry as I thought I was, and it appeared neither was Bradley. While playing with a piece of steak with his fork, again he looked straight at me and said in a very serious tone of voice, "I did those things because I want to be viewed as one of the boys. I want them to like me and accept me as one of them." He pointed to my observation notes and continued, "That's what we did when I was a salesman!"

We talked for about an hour on how a manager provides the primary role model subordinates emulate. At this point I asked Bradley if he felt his actions and behavior in Las Vegas provided the exact type of "professional" role model he was expecting from his salesmen. He never really answered the question, but it was obvious his wheels were turning…

About halfway through the carrot cake we each had for dessert, Bradley stopped chewing. Before swallowing (I knew he didn't swallow before talking because my left hand, along with the table cloth, got showered with moist food morsels), he said in an overly apologetic voice, "I never took a course in how to be a manager in college. The company never sent me to any management programs either. In fact, my eight years as a territory salesman did little to prepare me for *management*."

Déjà vu! Why did that little voice in my head take me back to those recruiting days when I heard from just about every applicant, "I would like to gain a little *experience* and then eventually move into *management*."

That was one evening I'll never forget! I periodically ask myself if I was the type of role model and sounding board Bradley needed that night. I think so; the house wine each of us had cost only $3 a glass...

Ever since that night, our personal and work relationships have developed and matured in a very positive way.

Chapter IV

Follow the Leader...

Ah well! I am their leader, I really ought to follow them!
Ledru-Rollins 1807-1874

The image of the American farm... For some it's what dreams and memories are made of. For others, it's a way of life. For me, it was a little of both. No, I can't reminisce about getting up every morning with the sun, doing chores, and taking care of the animals before going to school. Nor can I talk about working late into the evening during planting and harvest season. In fact, I can't even brag, like my father always did, about having to walk five miles barefoot to and from school each day in the snow and rain. On top of that, according to him, it was uphill both ways! As farm life is usually depicted on television, we did eat well, while the Walton's had nothing over our dinner table conversations. Maybe the name of our farm can best describe the type of rural lifestyle we experienced. Some of the surrounding farms had names like the "Rocking R," "The Ponderosa," and the "Two Bars Three." The last one didn't serve any alcoholic beverages! The name of our farm was the "Tax Deduction." You see, my father was a businessman, one of those white-collar professionals with his business and offices in town, while my mother took care of the home, family matters, and three children. I think her job was probably a little more challenging than my Dad's, she had the three of us kids to raise.

The "Tax Deduction" was comprised of approximately fifty-four acres of mainly rolling hills we called "The Land." The large, white two-story farmhouse had a big covered porch three quarters of the way around it. The barn at that time, and especially for three little kids, seemed to be the biggest man-made structure in the world. Talk about a wonderful place to play, no matter what the weather. The orchard was situated on top of a hill west of the house. You can call a dozen apple trees an orchard, can't you? I understood later in life that for tax purposes twelve trees could be called an orchard. The family garden had the usual domestic crops like tomatoes, a row of corn, lettuce, onions, and various and sundry experiments and research projects my two sisters and I periodically tried growing as part of our 4-H or scouting projects. Oh, and I almost forgot about our livestock herd which consisted of one cow, a couple sheep, an annual pig, chickens, two dogs, who knows how many cats, and an assortment of various pet rabbits, hamsters, fish, turtles, and anything else the three of us kids managed not to kill. Crops? Sure we sort of had them, too. Our neighbor, Mr. Harvey, leased about ten of our flat acres and planted buckwheat on it. Interesting how Mr. and Mrs. Harvey always had their freezer filled with venison, considering all the cattle they had and the fact that Mr. Harvey never had a hunting license. It really wasn't until I got my first full-time job after graduating from college that I fully developed an appreciation for the name of the farm, especially around April 15th.

Enough about the actual farm itself, more memorable are some of the lessons learned while living the "rural" life which have stayed with me to this day. We learned to value friends and neighbors, appreciate all living things, to observe firsthand the delicate balances within the environment, responsibility, independence, and all those other things everyone attributes to the traditional American farm.

One benefit of growing up "rural" has been the fine-tuning of our skills in observation and patience. Sitting on the farmhouse porch in the evenings provided the opportunity to talk, marvel at the wonders of Mother Nature, and perfect the ability to ask questions about the meaning of life and other important things, right there from our front row center seats to the world. I remember very distinctly, as if it were yesterday, the conversations of many an evening. The part of the porch where we liked to congregate on those warm summer evenings looked out over Mr. Harvey's pasture, where he had approximately seventy-six head of cattle. Invariably, it seemed whenever one of the animals started randomly walking in any direction, all the other animals would follow, even if it was just to crowd against the fence at the opposite corner of the pasture. It didn't even have to be feeding time. Eventually, another animal would start wandering away from the crowded corner, and, sure enough, all the others would follow till again they ended up closely huddled elsewhere in the pasture. Over the years I've asked many so-called experts, but have never heard anyone satisfactorily explain why such behavior occurs. Somehow as kids, we came to the conclusion that in the genetic hierarchy of brain and reasoning power, our cats and dogs were a little smarter than those cattle, even though their heads and brains were smaller. Just look at the size of a cat's or dog's head versus a cow's; talk about deductive reasoning abilities! There were a few anomalies in our theories. As kids, we did have some difficulty trying to understand why the cats and dogs, along with all the other animals, wanted fed one hour earlier in late October, after the clocks were set back an hour from Daylight Savings Time to Standard Time...

Personal Values

The informal day-to-day education we got on the farm served as a great foundation for my sisters and me as we pursued our individual career goals and life's aspirations. Mom and Dad retired on the farm but eventually had to sell "The Land" because the work of keeping after it was becoming a little too much for them to handle. Another reason had something to do with limited tax implications after retirement. Each of us kids went our separate ways in pursuit of our own share of the American dream. I'm constantly reminded of those early years on the farm by what I observe, experience, and usually question, in the business and corporate world.

It was my third day at the office and so far I was successfully fulfilling the duties of my new job. As you might guess, it was well within the "Gee, I didn't know that" grace period for any new employee. I've learned over the years that the "I didn't know that" grace period for "corporate" managers is substantially shorter than for a summer intern or even a full time administrative assistant. I'll bet I could graphically plot the mathematical relationship between the length of the "Gee, I didn't know that" grace period and the level of any position on the company organizational chart.

Being one of the first people to arrive at the office the morning of my third day, I had the choice of selecting any parking spot among the one hundred twenty-three or so slots that were available. My early arrival was not intended to impress anyone during my first few days in the new job. I'm just an early morning person and I always get to work early. Pulling into the parking lot, I unconsciously chose what I considered to be the *best* spot. The parking slot I chose was at the farthest corner from the building entrance. My reasoning went something like this. First, most people like to park as close to the door as possible. Second, I take pride in keeping my vehicle immaculately clean and scratch free. Third, my extended cab long-bed pickup truck takes up a lot of space. And finally, the little extra exercise I get walking to and from the building helps to compensate for the limited physical activity I get with a sedentary office job. Following that same line of thought, I usually don't wear coats during the winter, assuming I can burn more calories as my body tries to stay warm walking across the parking lot.

My manager stopped by my office on his way back from his early morning trip to the employee kitchen. On a daily basis, I could set my watch, almost to the microsecond, when he went for his coffee. Should the atomic clock in Greenwich ever malfunction, my manager's daily routine could be used as the backup. Now, he's a rather diplomatic type of person and I'm sure he handled the confrontation well, but he told me he was informed, while pouring himself a cup of black coffee, that one of his direct reports, meaning me, parked his "old truck" in another person's private parking space.

Seems Bob Spencer, the VP for Marketing, whom you'll hear more about later, in no uncertain terms told my manager that this was the "third day in a row" that it happened.

I started to laugh and fortunately my manager saw great humor in it, too. Obviously, Bob Spencer never lived in New York or any other major metropolitan city where parking spaces are at a premium. It was only three days into my tenure at the company, so logically my manager hadn't yet shared, nor had I been able to pick up or deduce, his opinions about some of the personal idiosyncrasies of other "corporate" colleagues. No, I didn't go out and move my truck! In fact, I intentionally have parked in that same spot since starting with the company, and have yet to have Bob Spencer personally mention a word to me about it. This incident served as the stimulus for focusing my "farm boy" observation and inquiry skills toward the

Personal Values

"corporate" parking behaviors. Sure enough, within a week, I learned that unless an unsuspecting visitor unknowingly occupied "someone's personal parking spot," you would see the same vehicles in the exact same slots every day. Okay, so what that I was doing the exact same thing. I was doing it for educational, and spite, purposes! Even if another colleague was on vacation or traveling on business for the day, "his or her" slot usually remained unoccupied the entire day. Whenever I mentioned to others, still during my new employee *grace period*, there seemed to be an informally assigned parking system, they would emphatically say there wasn't. Maybe I should've said "formally assigned" instead of "informally assigned." Then why was it the topic of extensive discussion if, God forbid, a vehicle was out of place? Did I mention that only sixty-one of the one hundred twenty-three spaces were actually needed on a daily basis? To use "chicken farm" terminology, what a pecking order...

Spring on the farm was always an exciting time of the year, with calves and lambs being born (not ours), new kittens and puppies, and all of our 4-H peers excitedly talking about their new baby animals. According to all the children, including my sisters and me, every newborn animal was eventually going to win a first place ribbon at the county fair or farm show. The growing, discovery, and learning process for young animals is extremely interesting to watch, and sometimes difficult to understand for little children. One example might be when a kitten learns from its mother to catch prey. They seem to learn and experience a sense of pleasure and satisfaction in torturing and playing with the catch before killing it, thus letting it die what to many of us seems like an agonizing death. That instinctive discovery and learning process, which for many of us seems to be irrational behavior, is quite similar to what happens in "corporate" America, and we accept it as rational. For me, the rationale for some of the learned behaviors in corporate America is as difficult to understand as those that motivate the cat with a mouse.

Part of my personal orientation to the company, and as a firsthand way to better understand how the organization actually functions, I scheduled a weeklong trip to visit a number of the geographically dispersed manufacturing sites. While at the various locations, I'd schedule appointments to meet with most of the operations managers and try to introduce myself to a majority of the supervisory personnel.

I wondered if anyone would consider taking *my* parking place while I was gone...

Knowing I would be out of the office for the entire week, I figured it would be prudent on my part to tie up a few loose ends before departing. Unfortunately those loose ends couldn't be tied up by the end of Friday afternoon of the week before my trip. So, being a morning person with nothing urgent planned for Saturday morning, I arrived at my usual 6:45 to 7:00 time slot. It was "casual dress" Saturday, like every Saturday and Sunday are. The office was very quiet and I could hear strange building sounds I hadn't heard before, mainly because no one else was in the building. Great! Now I could clean things up real quickly without interruptions and get on my way. Around 7:45 I heard a little shuffling noise down the hall, but figured someone else was in the same situation as I, with too much in the "in box" and too little week left. John walked by my office, casually said hello and started chatting about nothing in particular, while remaining standing in the doorway. His behavior seemed a bit unusual to me because John's usually very focused and businesslike in all the other contacts I've had with him. Around the office, his nickname is "The Hawk." Seems he got that nickname because he's usually very intense and acts like a hungry hawk that just spotted dinner. At least that's the way he is Monday through Friday.

Without John knowing it, Mitch suddenly appeared behind him and jokingly shoved him into my office, saying something nasty about John always blocking the doorway. Mitch now claimed occupancy rights to my doorway as John leaned against the wall. It was at this point I realized the rest of the office was buzzing with people. There was a noticeable difference between this "Saturday" buzz versus the Monday through Friday buzz. What's going on here? Was this the annual "clean out your desk drawers and recycle paper day" that I didn't know about? This "Saturday" buzz was rather casual, in fact, very casual. Instead of quietly doing "business" things in their individual offices, people seemed to be making a concerted effort to see and be seen. Both John and Mitch left my office after about eight minutes of chewing the fat and went into an office two doors down from mine. It sounded like they were successfully doing the same thing in Fran's office they did in mine – absolutely nothing.

Considering all the people who were in the building, I had to glance at my calendar for a second time just to make sure it was Saturday. Yep, it was Saturday all right, but why was the office so crowded? In my recent past, no, let's say for close to three decades, I've never seen an office, at least one that I've worked in, filled to seventy-five percent capacity on a Saturday. Bewildered and probably more confused than usual, which doesn't take much, I decided to disguise my exploratory mission to discover what was going on, as a trip to the men's room. I was determined to find out what the Saturday morning attraction was. Pretty clever, huh? To my amazement, people were gathered in groups of two and three in various offices as I walked down the hall in the direction of the rest rooms. Most of the conversations I briefly overheard seemed to focus on nonwork related topics like kids, sports, family, cars, and anticipated Saturday afternoon activities. In those few offices where I did notice single occupants, they appeared to busy themselves with newspapers, magazines, straightening piles of papers on their desks, aligning pencils, while in one office, a woman was watering and tending to a row of flowers perfectly arranged on her window sill.

On my way back from the men's room, which I didn't use, I noticed Jim Corbett sitting at his desk with what appeared to be a bored look on his face, with his body posture conveying the same message. The top of his desk was empty except for a pen and blank writing pad. Here's my opportunity to ask a trusted sixteen-year veteran of the company about what's going on. As I walked toward his door, I could tell by Jim's nonverbals I was more than welcome to enter his office and make myself feel at home, meaning stay a while. Jim's office gave me the feel of professionalism which matched his general everyday demeanor. I didn't know Jim very well, but there was something about him I liked. He seemed down to earth, not like a lot of the other "corporate" managers; he was not artificial and had what seemed like a realistic perspective on things. When his name would come up in conversations, you could tell others liked him too.

"Well, how's the new kid on the block doing?" Jim asked. We continued to "break the ice" and practice the standard rituals of establishing rapport for a few more minutes. Jim mentioned something about an upcoming project he was working on where he might be asking for my help. At that point in the conversation, I probably would have unconsciously agreed to anything he suggested because I wasn't really listening to what he was saying. I was trying to figure out how to switch the topic of our conversation to an explanation of this apparent Saturday morning office social gathering. Jim helped me out by suddenly asking "…and what are you working on this beautiful Saturday morning?" I told him about my following week's business travels and my obsessive-compulsive need to clean off my desk before I left. In turn, I asked him the same question. As Jim started to talk, I said to myself, "Yes! Finally I may have found a lead and possible answer to the Saturday morning buzz."

Jim's window overlooked the one hundred twenty-three space parking lot, and what a view it was, too. The parking lot had a lot more distracting activity compared to the monastic solitude of the courtyard my office window faced. Not only was he high enough to see the entire lot, but the walkway to the building came directly in front of his window. Jim said over his sixteen-year tenure with the company, he's observed a very interesting phenomenon in human behavior that faithfully occurs every Saturday morning, observable right outside his window. He had a front row seat. Seems most of the marketing department personnel show up on Saturday mornings approximately ten to fifteen minutes before the VP for Marketing, Bob Spencer, arrives. Then the reverse happens, but in a more compressed time period. After Bob leaves, those workers from the marketing department also disappear, but all within about a five-minute time frame instead of the lengthy ten to fifteen minutes when arriving. "Take a look and I'll show you!" Jim said as he pointed out the window to a man walking briskly away from the building towards the parking lot.

"Who's that?" I asked.

"That's George Hammer, the VP for Manufacturing," Jim replied, as he added, "just keep watching."

I didn't notice Jim glance at his watch as we peered out the window, but before George's car was down the access road and out of sight, a group of three other people exited the building. Anxiously watching the parking lot exit and making sure George's car was out of sight, they quickly hustled toward their cars. Jim said in a sarcastic voice, "Hmm, they're slow today! Took them forty-three seconds today instead of their usual thirty-five." Jim explained the three in the party were all direct reports to George.

Having a scientific mind and finding this one sample of "corporate" behavior, and what it implied, hard to believe, I suggested they might have had a emergency manufacturing meeting scheduled for this morning. Maybe they were all just leaving such a meeting together. "No, not at all!" Jim replied, quickly adding the comment, "You walked down the hall this morning, didn't you? And how many formal meetings did you see taking place?" We sat there talking for approximately thirty more minutes and during that time we observed the same scenario played out with the Human Resources Department, Public Relations, and the Accounting Group. "This has been going on since I've been here, and, I understand, for many years prior to that," Jim declared. He continued with, "Somewhere in the past, the act of showing up on Saturdays seems to have gained the connotation of "being dedicated and productive," you know, the company man type of behavior! The opposite, of not showing your face on Saturdays, seems to have acquired the connotation of being "lazy and unproductive." Nothing productive ever gets done on Saturday mornings, but everyone thinks they need to show up for some stupid but compelling reason."

"So nothing productive ever gets done on Saturdays?" I repeated, both as a question and a statement. Jim glanced over his glasses in that "are you kidding me" kind of look. "Okay! Okay! I see what you said," was my reply. Jim laughed what seemed to be a forced sarcastic laugh then said everyone, the VPs included, knows the "Saturday Matinee" is a political game, but they all willingly participate. As we talked about some of the ramifications, and some horror stories supposedly from Saturday Matinees gone by, the parking lot quickly

Personal Values

emptied. Over the years, Jim calculated that the VPs probably stayed, on the average, slightly *less* than one hour each Saturday. Their direct reports generally stayed, on the average, slightly *more* than an hour, several minutes prior to and after the VPs' arrival and departure times.

Jokingly, Jim said, "Like so many other things in life, timing is everything!"

It was about eleven o'clock and a lot later than I'd anticipated staying that morning. We said something about getting together soon to play a round of golf or have dinner together with our wives. I'm not sure if that was idle chatter or not, because we've said it before and have never done it. Then to put closure to our morning's discussion, as I was walking out of his office, I turned to Jim and asked him in a voice that I intended to be joking, but it probably came out quite serious, "Jim, then why are you here this morning?"

His reply was, "I guess I'm a political animal and follow the crowd. No sense in taking chances with my career..."

After checking my voice mail for one last time and placing several post-it notes of things I needed done next week on my secretary's computer monitor, I slowly walked out to my truck. About half way from the building to my truck, I started to visualize Mr. Harvey's cattle walking across the parking lot...

Chapter V

The Generation Gap

Like that of leaves is a generation of men.
Homer 8th Century B.C.

As a successful businessman, at least in our family's opinion, my father was the epitome of *practical*; almost to the point of his practicality being an obsession with him. I'm sure having grown up during the "Great Depression" left its mark on him, and on my mother too, but to a lesser extent. In no way do I intend to minimize the personal suffering and numerous problems people endured back then. Many lives and families were torn apart and life was unquestionably tough for just about everyone during that period of time. In all probability and as a direct result of his experiencing the Great Depression, my father was one of those individuals who believed in getting his money's worth out of everything he did or owned. My wife periodically reminds me that I seem to have acquired some of those same "practical" traits. Could it be genetic?

I remember a 1948 Hudson my father owned. It was a two-door businessman's coupe with a two-tone blue paint job. For

Personal Values

me the car was one of those inanimate objects that had many positive memories associated with it, probably because it played an integral part in many happy experiences during my formative years. I loved to sit in the front seat between my father, who was naturally driving, and my mother, who never let me sit by the door. I think it had something to do with her maternal fear of going around a turn, the door flying open, and her only son tumbling out of the car directly into the path of an oncoming tractor trailer. In looking back and considering the car, the probability of that happening was quite high. My sisters were delegated to the large back seat where they were usually quite content. In the 1950's, neither seat belts nor child restraint laws existed, so my normal traveling position was resting my chin and both hands on top of the solid metal dashboard while both my legs straddled the center floor hump. Can't really say much about being comfortable, or safe according to today's standards, but what a view I had looking out across the long hood...

As most of us mature and reach the age of reason, whatever that is, we would probably agree with the conclusion that there is generally a finite life expectancy for most material things, especially a car. My father had what appeared to be an insatiable urge to stretch life expectancies of every possession to the limit, not to mention his need to save what most people would consider trash. According to him, you never know when an empty tuna can might come in handy.

When it rained, hip boots and golf umbrella were standard equipment for *all* passengers inside that 1948 Hudson, assuming you didn't want to get soaked. Water leaked all around and through the windshield seals. At times, if all other windows were included in the calculations, the volume of interior water equaled or surpassed the gallons per second rate of Niagara Falls. In the winter, slush and cinders splashed up from the road through strategically positioned portals caused by the rusted out floorboards. The mildewed carpet remnants that covered the floorboard holes usually prevented passengers from getting dizzy from staring at the passing pavement underneath their feet. The carpet remnants also helped to prevent splashing water, road debris or serious injuries much above the passenger's knees. Dad's philosophy of getting his money's worth was applied to just about everything he, or we, owned. We suspect he was the ghost writer for the book entitled "Get Your Money's Worth."

We celebrated with a three-layered cake purchased from the local bakery the day my father finally decided to invest in a new sofa, along with several other pieces of upholstered furniture, for the customer waiting room at his business. From my recollection, the original furniture he had in the customer waiting area at the office was covered with a dark burgundy colored fabric, typical of office furniture back then. I don't know exactly what kind of fabric it was, but if it were up to my dad, rough unbleached burlap would have been fine. Through personal experience, I can attest that if you squirmed on the sofa even a little too much, you were guaranteed getting second degree brush burns, right through your clothes, not to mention strategically placed burgundy stains on your pants. Long after the end of what might be considered a sofa's practical lifetime, and even though the fabric was faded, streaked, and completely disintegrated after decades of ultra violet exposure from direct sunlight, my father still insisted the old sofa had a little bit of life left in it. The final crowning blow came the day a customer sat down on the sofa and suddenly let out an agonizing scream! Due to the dry rot of the fabric and severely stressed internal support system, and in all probability the stress imposed by what I understand was a rather robust woman, the sharp end of a coil spring struck like the fangs of a cobra. Thank goodness it was in an era when people weren't as litigious as they seem to be today. Dad never did tell us exactly where the lady got bit...

Personal Values

Over the years, I started to realize what my father positioned as his being "practical," today I would call resisting change. I remember when I was doing my undergraduate work at The Pennsylvania State University back in the 60s, Texas Instruments Inc. just introduced to the market a revolutionary product, an electronic calculator. What an innovative tool for calculating mathematics problems. It was a first of its kind with a red display of about six digits, a stationary decimal point, and no batteries. You had to plug it into a small transformer to make it work. Back then, an instrument that could only do simple addition, subtraction, multiplication, and division seemed rather awesome. Today the freebies found in cereal packages have more capability and capacity than that one did. In fact, I think I still have it somewhere in the attic. See, maybe the need to save things is genetic! Back then, the particular model I decided I needed and couldn't live without had a price tag of $137 plus Pennsylvania sales tax. Back then, $137 plus 5% sales tax was a lot of money, but I reasoned such an investment would more than pay for itself in the long run. Even when I was a sophomore in college, I anticipated going on to graduate school and continuing my education in the field of research and statistics. I had no concept of how fast technology would change and improve.

During a weekend visit home, as I was anxiously telling my father about the merits of this great electronic calculator I was planning on purchasing as an investment in my future, he quickly disappeared into the den. After several minutes he returned and very proudly handed me a used slide rule still in its original leather sheath. He proudly announced he used it when he was in school and was now honored to pass it on to his only son. He said he had another one he could use. The anticipation of owning my own personal electronic calculator was quickly fading away. How do you tell your father you don't want his thoughtful gift?

Dad pointed out that the leather sheath the slide rule snugly fit into had a reinforced oversized loop that made it easy to attach to one's belt. For whatever reason, he didn't seem to understand that on campus, only some of the agriculture and engineering students had those things hanging on their hips. Now was the time I probably should have asked if, by chance, he had any plastic pocket protectors he could spare for his wonderful son. Math majors proudly displayed them in their shirt pockets, usually encasing an assortment of pens and pencils. Even with his business, my father never did purchase or consider using an electronic calculator. In fact, I think his abacus was part of the inventoried items that went with the sale of his business when he decided to retire.

There was one thing Dad could never part with when he sold the business. I might add the basement was full of many other "treasures" he could never part with either. His prized possession was an "original" *Underwood* typewriter. I use the term "original" literally. I think Gutenberg used something similar to it! Talk about the "Days of Enlightenment!" The machine weighed at least seventy-five pounds, required a team of horses to move it, and when Dad started pecking away on that mechanical monster, seismographs within a fifty-mile radius would record the shock waves. Over the years, he became rather proficient at using his own "hunt it and press it" keyboarding system. Dad and his black behemoth made noises some rock music lovers of today might consider gold record material. For his birthday one year, my sisters and I wanted to get him a new electric typewriter. This was before laptops were even glimmers in any inventor's mind. The daily local TV reports about false tremors and earthquake echoes being recorded on seismographs around the county were starting to get embarrassing. After retirement, he enjoyed writing what he called his memoirs, along with writing detailed hour by hour summaries of all the trips and vacations Mom and he took. He

Personal Values

adamantly refused to even look at an electric typewriter. Years later, we again concluded a new word processor or computer, as a gift for him, was definitely out of the picture.

My father was not atypical from many of the people I see in business and industry today. Maybe they're not at the same extreme as my father was, but some of those same latent tendencies regularly show up. Sadly, many of the people I see today with the same attitudes toward innovation and change aren't even close to my father's age.

Whenever I travel for business, I make it a habit, or at least I make an effort, to combine several tasks into one trip. In addition, if I should need to visit with a customer for any reason, I like to spend the preceding day riding with the sales rep who services that account. That way I can get caught up firsthand with the status of the account. I can then prepare for any potential concerns, problems, or issues I may not have been aware of concerning the customer. Last, but definitely not least, I informally provide feedback and input to the sales rep on his performance while I'm riding with him.

Most of the sales reps regularly request I spend several days a year individually traveling with them if at all possible. They say they sincerely appreciate feedback on their performance from someone other than their manager. My approach is not to provide answers or spout bits of "corporate" wisdom. I prefer asking probing questions the entire time I travel with them. In fact, one sales rep commented to his sales manager that by the end of the day, he felt like the "Grand Inquisitor" was riding with him. Believe it or not, to me that was a compliment! That same sales rep further explained that I wasn't making value judgments about him or his performance. In a non-threatening way, I was making him think about his sales performance, along with many other things he might not have otherwise examined.

Andy Barnes was a territory sales rep with over twenty-eight years of experience in the industry. He was part of the sales force for a company that was acquired during a merger approximately twelve years ago. His manager and I were talking one day over the phone about another unrelated matter when I mentioned I would be riding with Andy, in his territory, the following week. Lee Monroe, who was Andy's sales manager, said with a noticeable sense of frustration in his voice, "Great, and I hope you can straighten him out!" It didn't take a genius to tell from his voice Lee and Andy were experiencing some, how should I say it, "obvious differences of opinion."

"You don't sound too pleased with Andy," I responded. As I said it I realized what a really dumb comment I'd just made. The Statue of Liberty could have deduced Lee wasn't very happy with Andy. I later rationalized the comment, at least in my mind, as my way of empathizing with Lee.

"You know, Bryan," Lee continued, "even though Andy is a middle of the pack performer and his sales goals and objectives are generally met, I have to wonder if he really has twenty-eight years of experience or if he has one year repeated twenty-eight times." Rather than explore Lee's concerns about Andy over the phone, and potentially bias my opinions, I suggested after I rode with Andy, Lee and I could get together. Maybe after riding with Andy I could more effectively help Lee by sharing some of my thoughts and observations. In reality, that was always my approach when riding with a sales rep. I would always inform the sales rep up front that I would provide and share feedback not only with him, the sales rep, but also with his manager about our visit. Lee sounded satisfied with the

Personal Values

arrangement and said he looked forward to getting my thoughts and insights.

As a sales manager, Lee is one of those individuals any corporation would consider a "high potential" employee. He's in his early thirties, well-spoken, enthusiastic, creative, innovative, shows leadership capabilities, demonstrates high energy, and as a sales manager could probably sell ice to an Eskimo at premium prices. Someday in the not too distant future, he could probably be considered for transfer in some capacity to the "corporate" office. For whatever reasons still unbeknownst to me, it seems all "high potentials" have to do a tour of duty at the "corporate" office. The tour is usually positioned as an "investment in their career." It seems to be some kind of cultural rite of passage.

Andy's territory, which was located in the Midwest, was comprised of long term, well-established customers. He knew his customers very well, and why shouldn't he, considering he'd been servicing the same people for his twenty-eight year career in sales. It was obvious from all of our customer visits during the day we spent together, that Andy was well respected and liked. There was a strong personal bond between him and all his customers. The demographics of Andy's typical customer was fifty-five to sixty years old, conservative white male, with a history of having been in the industry throughout his entire career. Andy also socialized with many of his customers, not only as a sales person in a business relationship, but also as a personal friend and neighbor.

I quickly noticed Andy had developed a very methodical and effective approach to all his sales calls. He documented for me how he always had his week planned well in advance with all appointments scheduled and neatly marked on his weekly calendar. He had a written call sheet for each appointment that always included his call objective, topics to be discussed, outcomes, and follow-up items. He was well-organized and prepared for every call, not only for the day we were riding together, but also for several weeks, if not months, in advance. It was obvious he wasn't trying to put on a "dog and pony show" for my benefit. Not only did Andy use a systematic sales approach, he was also very conscious and concerned about the professional image he projected, from dressing one step above his customers to having his automobile clean and well maintained, and everything in between. His social skills, etiquette, and demeanor would easily let him blend in with the British Royal Family.

For me, the day spent with Andy was very refreshing – it's great to see a *true professional* using and applying his skills. By late afternoon when all his previously scheduled appointments were completed, I suggested having his wife Noreen join us for dinner at a restaurant of their choice, my treat. He said Noreen would be working until about six o'clock, but he felt sure she would enjoy the opportunity to go out for dinner. Any break from the routine for her was always appreciated. We had about an hour before Noreen would get off work, so Andy suggested we go to his home office and wait for her there. That way he could check his mail and clean up a few odds and ends in the office. Such an arrangement was fine with me.

This was the first time I had the opportunity to be a guest at Andy's home office. His home was located in a very quiet bedroom community where all the homes were extremely well maintained with immaculate landscaping. Andy's office was what appeared to have originally been a spare bedroom on the first floor. The office was very tidy, well organized and conservatively decorated. Everything, and I do mean everything, was clean and orderly. I sat down at a spacious worktable while Andy proceeded to his desk. He immediately phoned his wife to let her know about the dinner invitation for that evening. From the sound of his voice, the look on his face,

Personal Values

and a thumbs up hand signal intended for me, she was definitely pleased and more than willing to go.

I asked Andy if I could use his phone to call my office and retrieve any voicemail messages I might have waiting to be heard. I didn't want to wait till later when I got to my motel room to get that routine task out of the way. Sure enough, I had four new messages since I checked at lunch. As I was listening to the messages, Andy pulled open a filing cabinet drawer, removed several manila folders, and started making entries and inserting handwritten sheets I recognized from some of today's earlier sales calls.

Like a kick in the seat of the pants it finally hit me! Why hadn't I picked up "on the obvious" earlier in the day? With the phone cord tightly stretched from Andy's desk to my ear while trying to make a couple of notes on a tablet, again my eyes quickly started to scan his office. I was now specifically looking for something. That's it! My hunch was starting to prove true. In one corner of the office next to a bookshelf was a stack of what appeared to be four unopened boxes. The bottom three had the name "DELL" boldly printed in blue on their sides, while the smaller unopened box on the top had "AT&T" printed on the side.

About a year ago, Lee Monroe submitted a proposal to the Corporate VP of Sales for funding to implement an SFA system (Sales Force Automation) on a corporate-wide basis for all field sales reps. According to the original proposal he submitted, along with being a "Customer Sales Contact" management tool for each of the sales reps, the SFA would be integrated into a corporate-wide enterprise system. The technology would tie the individual field sales reps into the order processing systems, collections, production scheduling, warranty services, and even accounting and transportation. The field sales force could then function on "real time," thus assisting them to be more customer responsive, and efficient, with more time for face-to-face selling. According to Lee, the sales force was burdened and bogged down with what he and many sales reps called "Corporate Administrivia." Writing reports, tracking down internal problems, trouble-shooting, and dedicating time to "corporate" office work took away from their precious selling time.

Possibly without enough forethought and understanding by the Board of Directors, Lee's proposal was accepted, partially funded, and implemented as part of a pilot study with Lee's group. If I recall correctly, I think I remember someone telling me the initial implementation started about a year ago... So much for Andy's computer, what about the mobile phone? I looked again toward the corner where the boxes were stacked. Upon closer inspection, the "AT&T" box definitely appeared to be sealed without ever having been opened. So that's why Andy asked to use the phone at several customers' offices. His mobile phone was still in its original box, unopened. Along with the SFA system, the mobile phones were part of the approved "corporate" plan to automate the field sales force.

After erasing the voicemail messages I didn't need to archive with the electronic maiden, I gave the phone back to Andy just as he closed another folder and carefully returned it to one of the four-drawer file cabinets. Okay, now how should I approach this in a diplomatic kind of way? There were several thousand dollars worth of equipment in unopened boxes sitting in the corner of Andy's office. So I opened my mouth and waited to see what would come out. What finally came out was something like, "I see you received your new computer and mobile phone."

Andy slowly but intentionally put down his pencil, turned and positioned his chair and body directly towards me, then looked me straight in the eye. I swear I observed his pupils constrict,

Personal Values

even from about eight feet away. The needle on the tension meter in the room suddenly shot up, pegging itself in the red zone. Well, maybe the tension wasn't quite *that* high as Andy started to speak softly and deliberately.

"What do Lee and you "corporate" people want from me?" Andy asked. "Haven't I always met my annual sales goals? Didn't you say earlier today I use an effective sales approach with all my customers? Aren't my customers extremely pleased and satisfied with how I work with them?"

I'm sure he could have gone on and on, but he stopped, probably realizing that "...killing the messenger," me, would be of little value. I quickly concluded the computer and phone were "bad" topics to bring up, especially just before dinner.

We had about forty-five minutes before Noreen finally got home. Those were forty-five *long* minutes for me, all of which were taken up with a very serious discussion; mainly a one-sided one at that, Andy talking, me listening. Thank goodness he didn't use my father's classic approach; silence then repeating a mantra for forty-five minutes would've been fruitless, not to mention agonizing for me. Andy posed a number of valid points. He admitted he wasn't a "techno-geek" like Lee was, and that he had no intention of *ever* becoming one. He saw himself as an effective sales man, not a cyberspace cadet. He was not averse to applying technology to the job, but felt a little overwhelmed when four boxes suddenly arrived on his doorstep without ever being informed they were coming. After they arrived, no arrangements or accommodations were made for training on how to set up the equipment or use the software. Andy also felt committing the last three decades worth of information on each individual customer into a database was a waste of time and an unrealistic request from Lee. Andy then indicated that numerous times over the past year, he made a concerted effort and had asked Lee for help.

He requested training, but was supposedly told by Lee to just "start playing around with it and you'll pick it up." Finally, Andy asked the most bothersome, but crucial, question on his mind, "Aren't I adequately meeting and generally exceeding my sales numbers?"

I knew my role that day was not to convince Andy to change, because in all probability that wouldn't happen no matter what I might say. I did revert partially back into my comfort zone, the "Grand Inquisitor" mode, and quickly came to the conclusion Andy and Lee were at odds not necessarily on sales goals and objectives, but the implementation of a change process. They needed to work this problem out together.

Thank goodness Noreen arrived at exactly six o'clock. Dinner that evening was very good. The food was excellent and I intentionally kept the conversation focused on anything but sales and technology. I'm sure both Andy and I unintentionally exhibited a higher level of anxiety over our earlier conversation than either one of us cared to acknowledge. Throughout dinner, Noreen had to feel the frustration of an unfinished conversation both Andy and I were personally revisiting over and over in our minds.

Later that evening, safely back in my motel room, I plugged in my laptop and quickly wrote up a summary feedback sheet, like I usually do, for Andy. It was about a page and a half long and contained my usual three headings, "Strengths," "Opportunities for Improvement," and "Miscellaneous." I would mail a copy to Andy when I returned to the office and ask him to give me a call if he had any immediate questions or concerns. Before turning off my laptop, I e-mailed a copy to Lee. On the top of Lee's copy, I asked him to give me a call at his earliest convenience. It was important!

Personal Values

An insurance agent friend of mine once used an interesting term when we were casually talking about the topics of personal liability and insurance claims servicing. That term was "contributory negligence." Basically, it means both parties to the claim share, to some extent, the "fault" or responsibility for the situation. In this case it appeared both Andy and Lee shared responsibility for their impasse. Andy finding it difficult if not impossible to "change" and Lee finding it difficult to understand and successfully implement a change process.

After talking with Lee over the phone about a week later, I got the distinct impression Andy and Lee were still continuing on their collision course. There was probably nothing I would be able to do, short of a miracle, to get them to talk, let alone see the world from each other's perspective.

I wonder if I should have typed my trip report with Andy on my father's old Underwood typewriter...

Chapter VI

The Value of Diversity

> *Of such deep learning little had he need,*
> *Ne yet of Latin, ne of Greek that breed*
> *Doubts 'mongst Divines, and difference of texts,*
> *From whence arise diversity of sects,*
> *And hateful heresies.*
> *Spenser 1552-1599*

The United States has always been known as the world's melting pot and the land of unlimited opportunity. Its strength, power, and standard of living were developed from the contributions of those who arrived from all corners of the globe. Their reasons to come to the United States were many. Their dreams were generally the same, the opportunity for a *better life*. The outcomes of this "experiment in democracy" have been the envy of the rest of the world.

As a kid growing up in Western Pennsylvania, the realization that people were *different* was never an issue; it was an appreciated fact and way of life. In truth, the diversity and uniqueness of all the people who were our friends and neighbors made for an even richer and fulfilling childhood. Many of the children we played and went to school with, and the various families we socialized with, were first and second generation United States citizens. Most of the people in our community had roots predominantly from Eastern Europe, but the demographics of the town included individuals with ancestry from all over the world. There were more last names that ended in "...ski, ...sky. ...vitz, ...witz, ...sen," and "...a" than you can imagine. Many of the immigrants settled in or developed communities that easily identified their heritage, and in many cases, their theological beliefs. Pride of being an American showed in communities like "Polish Hill," "Little Italy," "Squirrel Hill," "North Side," "West End," and many others. But the pride of being American was paramount, especially on holidays, when American flags adorned almost every home.

Somehow over the years, that sense of American pride seems to have diminished somewhat. On Flag Day this past year, our home was the only one in our community that displayed a flag. Even more disconcerting that day was the number of neighbors, friends, and colleagues who asked *why* we had our flag displayed.

Holidays in Western Pennsylvania, no matter when they occurred throughout the year, were always a culinary delight, not to mention the parades and pageantry that displayed an appreciation for ethnic traditions and customs. Christmas and Easter were my favorite holidays! We lived in our own version of "EPCOT" decades before ground was ever broken near Orlando, Florida. Now don't get me wrong, there were problems and fierce competition, and in many cases open hostility, between the various ethnic and religious groups, but the underlying appreciation for people *who were different* was well rooted.

The little league baseball team I played on had more bi-lingual and tri-lingual players than it did one-language, English speaking kids. We probably could have established our own "Berlitz Language School" right there in the dugout between innings. In reality, we *did* share and learn "choice" words and phrases in different languages. When our parents and grandparents didn't want the kids to know what they were saying, or possibly were trying to keep a secret, they would speak it in their native or ethnic tongue. Even though our parents and grandparents didn't know it at the time, we learned and shared more naughty four-letter words, in various languages, than our parents could ever imagine. It's funny how kids back then, and even more so today, manage to pick up and understand what they're not supposed to! We also managed to become multi-cultural in our body language and hand gestures, also, in many cases, to the chagrin of our parents.

It seemed we all took great pride in our own ancestral differences and idiosyncrasies, while at the same time respecting and appreciating those things unique or different in others. Our little world was extremely heterogeneous, a real potpourri of diversity.

Over the years I've had the wonderful opportunity to travel domestically and internationally for both business and pleasure. For those fortunate to have had the opportunity to travel extensively, the exposure to the people, places, and the uniqueness of various countries and cultures instills a sense and appreciation for our vast worldwide community. I'm not sure who said it, but the phrase "I haven't met anyone that I haven't learned something from," definitely applies. Was it Will Rogers who said it?

There was about a ten-year period, while I was working with a large international corporation, that I was transferred and relocated eight times. For you analytical types, eight moves comes out to a new address on the average of every fifteen months. That's one way to keep from having unwelcome relatives visit, they never knew if you would still be at the same address by the time they completed their travel arrangements. For those of you who have relocated several times, you know the logistics of moving can be quite tedious and stressful, but in the overall picture of things, the benefits have been priceless. At the time, not all of the benefits were pleasant to bear, but looking back in perspective, they're experiences I, and probably you have cherished forever.

Texans, whether native or "wannabes" transplanted from other states, are very proud of their "big" state. And rightfully they should be, but for some individuals their pride borders on arrogance. In the late 70s, my transfer to the great Lone Star State placed me in a small town in East Texas. It was located about a two and a half hours drive east of the Dallas/Fort Worth Metroplex, about an hour southwest of Texarkana, and about two hundred fifty miles north of Houston. The name of the town was Lone Star, Texas. If you don't believe there's such a place, pull out your Triple A roadmap of Texas and look about thirty-five miles due north of Longview. That's where I developed a taste for one of their local culinary favorites, and what I personally now consider a delicacy: fried catfish, hush puppies, and a long neck. Fried catfish, East Texas style, doesn't appear on too many menus around the United States.

East Texas is not what one would classify as a traditional American ethnic melting pot. I realized that the first time I thumbed through the local Lone Star, and surrounding communities, phone book. The telephone book itself was about as thick as the Parade Magazine in the Sunday editions of big city newspapers. There were several pages of last names like Smith, Jones, Weaver, Garner, Wilson, Anderson, and Robinson. I didn't notice any of the "ski" or "itz" ending names I'd grown up with. In fact, I didn't find very many last names that might have even hinted to one's ancestry. Glancing through the yellow pages under churches or religion, one would quickly realize that the Baptist faith was predominant. I didn't see any Serbian or Greek Orthodox Churches listed, no Jewish Synagogues, nor any eastern religions represented. However, there was one listing for a Roman Catholic Church. The total yellow pages section in the phone book included approximately eighteen pages if you counted the index page.

Soon after arriving in East Texas, I asked one of my direct reports, who was a "native" Texan, and something taken very seriously by native born Texans, if she would be kind enough to take my wife and me on a "new comers" tour around the surrounding area. We wanted to get a general lay of the land, so to speak. Starting our tour early one afternoon, we approached a small town just north of Lone Star. I inquired about what appeared to be a large abandoned building off to the right side of the road. The large building, comparatively speaking for the area, appeared to have been abandoned fairly recently, probably within the last few years. Considering the building's easy access and proximity to the road, I wondered why it was empty and showing signs of recent vandalism. We were told the building was occupied and used until about three years ago. It was the *"Black"* school. Our tour guide, who was driving, emphasized the word *"Black."*

Certified as an elementary school teacher, my wife applied for a full-time teaching position at one of the local elementary schools shortly after we settled in. The elementary school she applied to was several miles from our new home. At the time, this part of East Texas didn't experience a lot of transferred professionals with highly qualified trailing spouses, especially ones who were certified to teach elementary school. Within a week after completing the application process, my wife was offered and readily accepted a position to teach second grade.

Personal Values

I arrived home before my wife did on her first day of teacher in-service. That's the fancy name given to the preparation and meeting days the teachers and administrators have a few days before the students arrive for the first day of class. When she arrived home late that afternoon, the first thing she asked for, no demanded, was a long neck, and it didn't matter if the beer was cold or not. Keep in mind, she had the temperament more similar to that of a wine connoisseur. Being astute in reading her non-verbal communications, I got the distinct hint there was definitely something troubling her. Without my having to inquire, she noticed my eyebrows raise and instinctively knew my gesture was the same as a question and request for her to expound, which she did.

Upon arriving at the school early the first day of teacher in-service, she was shown to her new room by one of the administrative assistants. As the administrative assistant opened the door and walked in with my wife right behind, my wife noticed a row of student desks conspicuously positioned against the outside window wall of the room. The one window-row of desks was separated from the rest of the room by what appeared to be an unusually wide aisle. In my wife's mind, the janitors probably forgot to reposition them after cleaning and waxing the floors over the summer break. After the assistant showed my wife the cloak room, closets, and how to operate the heating and cooling thermostat, my wife started moving the window-row desks closer towards the middle of the room and the rest of the desks. Instead of helping, and with a look of amazement on her face, the assistant said in a slow Texas drawl, "You might want to leave those there, they're for the *Black* students."

There were several empty long necks left on the kitchen counter as we turned the lights off to go to bed that night. I only drank a glass or two of wine that evening.

The Value of Diversity

Enough reminiscing, that was years and what seems like too many relocations ago.

Margaret and I were working together on a policies and procedures project that had potential long-term implications for not only my department, but for the department she was in as well. Considering the scope and possible ramifications of the project, our recommendations could affect the rest of the organization. Margaret was in her late forties to early fifties, and a very professional worker who was well respected throughout the company. She was a loyal and dedicated worker who reported through the department director. Even though it was still over a decade into the future, she openly admitted she was looking forward to retirement. Having worked for the company her whole career, she was a wonderful resource to ask historical perspective types of questions concerning the company and its operations. She was also a wonderful sounding board and resource when it came to making decisions that could have potentially adverse internal political implications. She knew the "corporate" political system, and how to use it, better than anyone.

We spent quite a lot of time together researching topics, discussing potential alternatives, and writing drafts of our policies and procedures recommendations and conclusions. During the time we worked together, she provided me with a number of helpful and relevant insights about the culture of the company. She posed to me a few hypotheses she developed about the corporation over her many years and challenged me to observe and see if I agreed or disagreed with her conclusions. I was still new with the company, so I took on her challenges as focal points to learn more about the organization, the culture, and the people that ran it. At first glance, her hypotheses seemed completely ill-founded.

Personal Values

Our office complex presents a rather plain but businesslike and professional image for anyone who visits the facilities. Much like any "corporate" building, the designing architect probably resurrected some long lost blueprints, rearranged several of the rooms, randomly added here and there a few accent colors and different brick façades, and then intentionally charged an exorbitant amount of money for the service. The main public entry is well-appointed with receptionist desk, oversized product and marketing pictures on the walls, and plush furniture in the adjacent visitors' waiting area. Meeting rooms and the restroom facilities are strategically positioned near the main entry to the building so visitors don't have to wander all over the facility when looking for the rest rooms. The executive wing, or *The Suite* as "corporate" residents on that side of the building like to call it, furnished with what looks like Ethan Allen furniture, provides lots of open space, and accommodates secretarial work stations that look like something Martha Stewart had a hand in designing and decorating. The appointments in *The Suite* and main reception areas are distinctive. The other wings, except for the outside wall windows and locking door manager's offices, have two-person collapsible cubicles crowded into what might be called *institutional décor*. I'm convinced the arrangement challenged the occupancy limits and fire codes of the city. The boardroom has the traditional long wooden table that totally dominates the middle of the floor. Mounted on the walls around the room are framed portraits of past and present board members, executives, and other randomly selected individuals. After reading some of their titles, I still have no idea why some of their pictures were there. Rumor has it that many of the people in the "random" and questionable portraits had some secret pictures of their own of various decision-makers. Isn't that called blackmail?

By just standing in the boardroom and looking around, I was suspecting Margaret was going to be right on the first of the seven challenges she posed to me. But before immediately giving in to her conclusion, I had to confirm her hypothesis by at least one other source of credible evidence. Like many companies, the "Directory of Executives and Management Personnel" provides a wonderful tool for analyzing some of the more obvious demographics of the company's management personnel. Many of the pictures that accompanied the short bios of each executive and manager appeared somewhat outdated or at a minimum, computer enhanced. It's amazing what photography, and computer technology, can do to disguise the effects of aging. Upon further examination of the Directory, along with soliciting inputs from several other trusted and well-informed sources, I came to the conclusion Margaret was absolutely correct on the first of her challenges. Just like she said, there were no women or minorities to be found on the board, in executive positions, VP positions, or even filling corporate management roles throughout the total corporation. I must add a disclaimer that the previous statement could be in error, because the blood lines and genealogy of each individual manager in the directory was not investigated. But from the perspective of "face validity," Margaret was absolutely correct.

Score so far: Margaret   1   Bryan   0

Six more hypotheses to go.

Performance reviews, in theory, should never pose any surprises, especially for the employee whose performance is being evaluated. In most companies, performance reviews are generally tied to salary increases and annual bonuses, just as they're rumored to be here. Over my long career in management or supervisory roles, I've experienced both easy and, in some cases, hostile performance reviews with subordinates. One observation I made that completely amuses me, however, is how an employee's performance and productivity seem to peak during the two months before and after the annual performance review. In any case, the way I like to view the performance review process is that it should be ongoing throughout the year. If there is a continuous open dialogue between the manager and employee, relative to performance and achievement of goals and objectives, both parties should correct or avoid any problems before, or as soon as, they occur. From what I've observed, so much for theory...

The way annual salary increases and bonuses were calculated is a book by itself. Managers in this company have perfected the skills of "sucking up."

Fortunately, when I was hired, I inherited a staff of very capable, experienced, and dedicated people. My compliments to my predecessor for having hired and developed such a fine team. He did a great job! At first, I observed and experienced the typical jockeying for position by subordinates that takes place when a new manager comes on board, but otherwise the transition went well.

For some unknown reason, we do our performance reviews about one month before we do annual budgeting. When I questioned the practice, I was told it was probably out of a long-standing tradition or habit rather than based in logic or perceived business necessity. The reason I questioned the practice was because the employee performance reviews are scheduled for completion during the peak season of our annual manufacturing and selling cycle. For a sales team with numerical goals and objectives, they either have to base attainment of their annual goals and objectives on the previous year's metrics or this year's incomplete metrics, or a combination of both. Even for manufacturing, employee performance reviews during the middle of the peak manufacturing crunch don't quite make sense to me. The same goes for most of the other departments as well, like customer and warranty services and technical support. Once I made the mistake of inquiring about the timing of the annual performance reviews and was quickly told "we've always done them in the past during this time of the year. Besides, the President thinks they should be done now! Are you going to question his wisdom?" Over the years, I've learned to select my fights carefully, and this wasn't one of those battles worth fighting or even exploring any further.

After the performance reviews were completed, working on the budget was the next mandatory administrative project that needed to be completed during the "peak season." Usually budgeting is a straightforward administrative exercise, at least when it comes to line items like salaries, benefits, travel, and operations numbers. Special projects and capital expenditures are another story! I was determined that by the end of the year I would automate most of my office procedures, including the budgeting process. The company's IS (Information Services) department was most helpful by already having standardized every type of company form that existed since the company's founding, including all financial and budget reporting processes. Supposedly we would be able to submit our budgets this year electronically. With my limited exposure to the accounting and IS departments, I was starting to wonder if I was working for a branch of the Internal Revenue Service.

In an effort to understand how to use the new electronic budgeting system, I set up an appointment to meet with one of the IS geeks who develops and specializes in corporate accounting and financial software. Believe me, I have no idea what his title was. There were six words in his job title, none of which I understood except possibly for the one that said "Software" something. During the meeting with the techno-geek, I discovered a software program existed where I could graphically plot the salaries of each of my employees. That's for me! What a great tool for doing projections, planning, and comparisons for internal and external parity. To me graphs are like pictures, worth a thousand words.

A day or two later when I started playing with the software, I became mesmerized by the program's capabilities. I had a great time manipulating the sample data, or "dummy data" as the geek called it, and printing every imaginable version of graphs and charts I could think of, and even some I couldn't think of. Within the program were weird correlation coefficients and statistical manipulations that could probably challenge last year's Nobel Prize winner in the field of multivariate analysis and fractals, if there was such an award.

After an hour or so of random discovery, and finally feeling comfortable with the software program, I started plugging in my department's "real" budget and salary data. To my surprise, no, let's call it shock, I quickly noticed a definite pattern emerging! Maybe I entered the data incorrectly? No, not at all. I double-checked and found my data entry was done correctly. Could I have stumbled into another one of Margaret's conclusions? Maybe!

The next day, I intentionally met Dennis Hall near the employee entrance to the building; you know the one that has a large sign painted on the glass that says "For Employees Only." What a great way to make visitors and customers feel welcome! Knowing the precise time Dennis leaves for lunch every day, I managed to be talking with another colleague "accidentally on purpose" near the door. As he passed by, I asked Dennis if he would be so kind as to stop by my office later that afternoon so I could share something interesting with him. I dared not tell him what that something was at this point or in ear shot of anyone else. Yes, the decision to talk with Dennis was well planned and calculated on my part. He had been with the company for about the same amount of time as I and was responsible for a department with almost twice the staff as mine. And to top it off, he was one of those computer freaks who liked to read and experiment with obscure computer language in the evenings, just for the fun of it.

Dennis stopped by my office around three o'clock, plopped himself down on the chair across the desk from me and with a half-chewed cookie still in his mouth said, "Whatcha wanna show me?" I told him about the software I'd received from IS that plots salaries and does all kinds of budgeting manipulations, and I thought he might like to see how it worked. That's like asking a kid if he likes ice cream. I waited until Dennis finished swallowing his cookie before I invited him around the desk to get closer to my computer. I have an aversion to having fresh food crumbs sprayed directly from the source all over me and my work area.

Dennis was impressed with the software and its capabilities. But like me, he became more intrigued with the results it produced with my department's data. Out of curiosity, he wanted to plug in the data for his own department to see if it would turn out the same way. In addition, he decided he could use the software to finalize his own department's budgeting process, which was due by next week.

The first thing the next morning with briefcase in hand, Dennis was at my door, even before he went to his own office. "You're not going to believe this, but look here," he said as he threw a pile of graphs and charts in the middle of my desk. There were even attachment sheets with handwritten formulas and extensive calculations. Dennis said, "The differences I found were statistically significant *even* at the .01 level of confidence." I don't know too much about significance levels at the .01 level of confidence, but any third grader could tell by looking at his graphs they were almost identical to mine. Dennis went on to say he intentionally stratified his data using a number of different variables, whatever that means, and again he got the same results.

I guess Margaret was right again! There were significant differences (Dennis' term) in the compensation levels of men versus women, minorities versus non-minorities, minority men versus non-minority men; minority women versus non-minority women, and a number of other comparisons Dennis invented or found. He even identified blatant and consistent differences in employee's compensation between groups of individuals with almost identical credentials, performance, and experience who were doing the exact same job. If such was the case for both Dennis' and my departments, could we assume the same was true elsewhere within the company?

Score to Date: Margaret   2   Bryan   0

Five more hypotheses to go!

Should I just concede and tell Margaret I'll take her word on the other five? If the other five are true, which I'm now convinced they are, I can understand why she's still in the low-level supervisory position she's in and can't wait to retire as soon as possible.

Maybe the next thing I should verify, which was not one of Margaret's conclusions, is if a majority of the executives, managers, and department heads are from East Texas...

Chapter VII

Short Term Personal Gain and the Price of a Popsicle

Light gains make heavy purses.
                    Bacon 1561-1626

Throughout life, it seems we're constantly placed in situations of making difficult decisions which position short-term personal gains against longer-term goals and objectives. In many circumstances, and maybe I should venture to say in most situations, the focus on long-term benefits usually produces greater returns than if we focus just on the short-term ones that usually benefit only ourselves. The need for many people to focus on short-term goals and objectives seems to be more a matter of being egocentric and personally self-centered. Maybe the tendency to be short-term oriented is a latent survival instinct carried over from the time when daily survival was paramount. I don't recall the topic ever discussed in my Psychology 101 or Sociology classes.

One of my earliest personal experiences with the short- versus long-term phenomena that stands out in my mind, even to this day, goes back to pre-school days, and that's many years ago. More years than I care to admit... This whole scenario is permanently etched in my brain forever. One of my two older sisters was about five years my senior while the other sister was only one year plus a few days older than I. As you might suspect, the bond between the sister that was one year older than I was significantly stronger than the bond with the sister with five years seniority. I'm not implying the three of us weren't emotionally attached and close with each other. On the one hand, we could argue and fight like hungry Russian wolf hounds, but, on the other hand, we would display the same level of intensity and unity in defending each other against someone else. Let's face it, my oldest sister, at age five, had better things to do with her time than to be bothered with a newborn baby brother. Even after our early years, why would a *high school junior* care to associate with, let alone admit she had a younger brother in elementary school? I must admit that when she started dating in high school, the differences between us got a little wider and our emotional bonds were regularly tested, particularly from her point of view! Okay, instead of our differences getting a "little wider," they got real wide, from both our perspectives! Little brothers and sisters didn't fit into the high school dating scene very well, not to mention the constraints and limitations imposed by conservative parents on the first born daughter. When my oldest sister went off to college, she considered a little junior high school brother one of the dorkyest things on God's good earth. At that time I didn't even rate, in her mind, the status of being human. Somehow though, over the years since then, the five-year spread in age between us has gradually become negligible, except when she's celebrating another one of her birthdays. To me, revenge is sweet; especially now, as practical "senior" jokes seem most appropriate. I have to concede she now tolerates my pranks quite well.

The one-year age difference between my other older sister and me was never a major problem. I must admit though, as with my oldest sister, I now take great pleasure, more than ever before, in emphasizing the one year age difference between us, especially around and on her birthday, especially milestone birthdays. It's fun, almost to the point of being obnoxious, to keep reminding her in various ways she's still my "older" sister. The connotation of "older" as I use it today is quite different than it was four decades ago. Sis and I were almost inseparable during our formative years. And even in college, when we both went to the same university, a sister was usually more of an asset than a liability when it came to the dating game.

I'm convinced every kid, as part of his normal growing up, maturation, and socialization process, either developed or belonged to an informal or impromptu "club" that served as a focal point in his life. I'm not talking about street gangs or, on the other end of the continuum, organized groups like scouting or 4-H. What I am talking about here are the fraternal bonds little children develop as part of membership and participation in a group with a common goal. My sister Sis and I, along with two first cousins, formed our own fraternal club. The dynamics and memories the four of us attribute to and associate with the club become more interesting, exaggerated, and nostalgic to reminisce about as we grow older. That only happens when we all get together, which isn't often enough. Getting together and visiting is like re-reading a favorite old book, watching for the ninety-eighth time a "Lassie" rerun, or looking at the family album and starting every sentence with "Do you remember when…" or "I remember the time that…" Come to think about it, when we do manage to get together, the conversation sounds similar to what might be heard on the front porch of a retirement home on a warm summer evening. Somehow, the more we exaggerate and embellish the stories,

Personal Values

the more we continue to believe them to be true. The myths are now becoming reality for us...

We developed the club, called the "Choosey Choosers," with a formalized organizational structure. We had elected officers, an unwritten mission statement, bylaws that were readily changed or modified, or more like ignored, to fit our changing circumstances. We even had a treasury with annual membership dues assessed on each member who was in good standing. The club provided a wonderful forum, without any of us realizing it at the time, for experiencing some of the realities and lessons of organizational life. The election of club officers was supposed to take place annually. In reality, the offices of President, Vice President, Secretary/Treasurer, and whatever other kind of position that seemed appropriate during the election process, usually took place on an as needed basis. "As needed" in this case meant during or immediately following a significant emotional event in *any* of the four club members' lives. Once, as an example, a "special" mid-term election was scheduled and held. A cousin, who was one of the club's four members, accidentally got hurt and unfortunately ended up being rushed to the hospital for medical treatment. From what I can remember, underwriter-approved bicycle helmets were not state or federally required safety equipment at the time. With the injured party in stable condition and recuperating at the hospital, an emergency meeting was called to order and a "special election" for officers of the club was conducted. That's one nice thing about an organization without a lot of layers of bureaucracy, things happen fast! With a majority of three out of the club's four members present, the injured member was quickly nominated and unanimously elected President. Prior to admittance to the hospital she was the club's Secretary/Treasurer. Thankfully, I never got injured seriously enough, nor did I experience any major trauma bad enough for any kind of sympathy, let alone get a special election scheduled on my behalf. Come to think about it, possibly because the club's gender mix tallied three girls and one boy (me), I *never* did get elected to the office of President, Vice President, or Secretary/Treasurer. I usually held the post of **Official Club Standard Bearer** or **Chairman of the Cleanup Committee**. I must have been the altruistic one in the club or extremely unaware of the group dynamics taking place, because I took great pride in just being part of the club. In retrospect, looking back on the club's political climate, I probably didn't realize what was going on or didn't know any better. The token positions I was usually elected or appointed to were probably more than I could have handled at the time anyway.

By today's standards, our treasury may not have sounded very impressive, nor would it have given much competition to the spare change in Bill Gates' pockets, but our Secretary/Treasurer took great pride in maintaining and balancing the club's ledger. If I recall correctly, our balance sheet never did show any numbers to the left side of the decimal point. The Treasurer's report and the balance sheet were always focal points for all our meetings, which were usually held on an impromptu basis. The balance sheet and all of the club's "hard" currency were kept secured in a screw-top canning jar. That jar and its contents played a major role in determining the club's fund raising and social activities. Collectively, and after a unanimous vote, which we thought procedurally complied with *Robert's Rules of Order,* we developed a long-term goal for the club and its four charter members. Through what we thought was diligent research and planning, hard work, along with appropriate investment strategies, we came to the conclusion a weeklong vacation to Disneyland (DisneyWorld didn't exist back then) was within the realm of viable possibilities. Surely, we reasoned, because all of us were official members of the *Mickey Mouse Club,* special group discounts would be graciously extended to our affiliate organization. I was most proud to be an integral part,

Personal Values

actually the primary financial contributor, of the fundraising process. The brainstorming and strategic planning efforts fell under the purview of the three *female* executive team members, while the hard work of fundraising came under my layman's jurisdiction. During one of our elections for officers, my name was on the ballot legitimizing my new title befitting such a responsibility. Seems I was the only one of the four club members who had a semi-steady income back then. As an elementary school entrepreneur, my income consisted of proceeds from helping the neighbor wash his car on Saturday mornings and keeping him and his wife entertained while they sat on their porch on many warm summer evenings. The cookies and other baked goods we ate while sitting on their porch were also well appreciated perks, but couldn't really contribute to the club's bottom line.

Somehow, that week long vacation to Disneyland never did come to fruition, at least as an organized club activity. Seems like there were always a number of other unexpected priorities that somehow took precedence. Not that we weren't all individually or collectively committed to our long-term goal of vacationing at Disneyland, but a number of shorter term priorities consistently seemed to get in the way.

After each formal club meeting, an impromptu social activity usually followed, just as many of the social and civic groups we belong to today, conclude with cake, coffee, and sometimes various adult beverages. The social activity at the end is usually the bribe or reward for members to sit through the business portions of the meetings. Our club meetings were generally held at our house or at my cousins' house when we all got together to play. Both locations were blessed with small corner stores not too far away. "Too far" in this case meant a safe walking distance for kids our age after parental approval was granted. Back then, corner stores usually had freezer sections and display areas dedicated exclusively to kids. You probably know what I mean. The display table, ice cream freezer, and merchandise racks were just our height with all those child priced goodies temptingly arranged precisely at eye level for our easy scrutiny. Talk about marketing, the storeowners knew exactly how to display their merchandise for our discriminating tastes. The freezer that housed the ice cream, and various other frozen treats, was always strategically located in close proximity to the cakes and candies. What a lesson in market place positioning and a nightmare for parents! After each club meeting, and for whatever unexplained reasons, the club's executive committee, made up of three females, usually came to the conclusion that Popsicles were the club's official food for the social event, at least during the summer months. During the winter months, the treasury was usually under tighter scrutiny because the neighbor didn't wash his car on a weekly basis nor did he and his wife spend much time on their porch. Talk about a great lesson on supply and demand cycles!

Our Secretary/Treasurer diligently recorded the twelve-cent expenditure after each outing. The rest of us watched closely as the ledger was updated and the remaining currency recounted before securely tightening the lid back on the Mason jar. Back then, each Popsicle cost six cents and could be conveniently split into two pieces, resulting in each of the club members sharing equally in the spoils of our (my) labor to the tune of three cents each.

The "Choosey Choosers" never made it to Disneyland, at least as an organized club function. It seems the immediate lure and pleasure derived from the dripping Popsicles was too much for all of us to resist. Without realizing it at the time, our behavior was probably one of our earliest lessons and exposures to *GroupThink*. This groupthink phenomenon as portrayed in this Popsicle story is not necessarily unique just to children. It seems to manifest itself to varying degrees at various stages

Personal Values

throughout our lives. Do you remember diligently studying on a Friday or Saturday evening in your dorm room while in college? Suddenly your good intentions got shattered because of a phone call or knock on the door by a friend suggesting a badly needed break from studying. The study break usually consisted of patronizing one of the local business establishments, and I'm not talking about clothes shopping. Even though you had a mid-term exam scheduled in statistics class the first thing on Monday morning, you rationalized joining your friends that night anyway. Why not, you still had the rest of the weekend to prepare for the test on probability theory and correlation coefficients. We've all done it!

Harley Rodman managed one of the company's core-business manufacturing facilities for the past seven years. He was a very dedicated worker, showing up before six o'clock every morning and never leaving for home until after six o'clock every night. Harley was one of those managers whom everyone aspired to be like. He enjoyed socializing and joking around with all the workers at the facility, while maintaining the reputation of being impartial and fair in how he resolved employee problems and handled requests. Even more important to "corporate" management was the fact he seemed to have a very good handle on his assigned manufacturing operations. As a result, his numbers showed his facility was consistently one of the best performers in most categories and metrics "corporate" managers looked at over the past five or six years when compared to the other manufacturing facilities. As an outcome of all their individual efforts, his team loved the production bonuses they regularly received for their collective performance.

One day last month, I had the opportunity to visit his operation(s) as part of a tour scheduled with representatives from a major international customer. Disguised as part of a new marketing program, the visiting customer representatives were invited to participate in a new product rollout and promotional scheme. The scheduled plant tour and a few promotional meetings seemed to satisfy the corporate "bean counters'" need to justify a planned round of golf one afternoon during the several day visit. Our bean counters reviewed and scrutinized every expense report the way a forensic medical examiner performs an autopsy for a high profile murder case. The bean counters always seemed to be mumbling something about tax implications and allowable expenditures when they reviewed our expense reports.

Harley did a great job in leading the plant tour, answering questions, and socializing with the customers. That's probably why sales likes to schedule customer tours at his facility instead of any of the others. Just after he eloquently answered the last customer question and as we started the process of boarding the bus again for our next stop on the tour, Harley came up behind me and said he'd like to talk about several service quality problems he was starting to experience. He probably planned and timed his comment to me, because he seemed to know what I would say even before I said it. "Sure, Harley, I would be glad to," I replied, continuing with, "In fact, if you're able to cut yourself free this afternoon about three o'clock, why not join us at the country club. We've got all our guests paired up for golf this afternoon, but the foursome I'm in is short a man. Would you like to join us? We could talk then." Do I need to tell you what his answer was?

When our tour bus, filled with anxious golfers, finally pulled up to the clubhouse, Harley was already at the driving range. He must have been there for some time considering there was less than half a bucket of range balls remaining in the extra large bucket next to him. I have never understood why golfers hit a large bucket of balls before a round of golf, or for that matter, why they take practice swings before every shot. Why waste

Personal Values

all that good form, energy, and potential great shots before actually hitting the ball?

We barely got fifty yards onto the fairway right off the first tee before Harley started talking, while feverishly looking for his ball he topped. Seems he was getting a little annoyed with the people from the Quality Control Department, not to mention his misdirected anger with the Big Bertha driver still in his hand. Considering the potential lethal weapon he was holding, I hoped his annoyance didn't spread to anything more than the golf ball. With an obvious hint of irritation in his voice, he continued speaking, "In the past, measuring production quality was easy. We knew exactly what to do, we did it, and everyone was happy. Now for some crazy reason, Quality wants us to change everything. Why? The quality of product coming off my floor is better than it's ever been. In fact it's better than any of the other manufacturing facilities anywhere in the company."

As I understood it, the corporation's Director of Quality Control, with the blessing of the executive team, had started to incorporate various new and innovative measures of customer satisfaction and loyalty into the formula used to calculate manufacturing quality. It wasn't going to be just product specifications and production statistics anymore. Harley sliced his second shot into the adjacent fairway as he lamented: "My job is to make a quality product and keep my operation running efficiently at full capacity. It's up to those sales and service people to keep the customers happy. What do they think they get paid for anyway?"

According to Harley, the quality control people were supplying the corporate office with production and customer service numbers that were significantly different from his. Supposedly, Quality Control and Harley were measuring the same things, but their numbers weren't even close. Among the major differences were metrics like "Orders Shipped on Time," "Orders Shipped Complete," and "Service/Warranty Response Times."

"Production used to be a lot of fun," Harley continued, "but now everyone else seems to butt their noses into where they don't belong, my operations. When was the last time you saw those "corporate" guys, or even quality control down on the floor in any of the plants, let alone mine? They like to sit in the office and gather numbers." Harley intentionally smacked the head of his club into the ground after topping his next shot. He was attempting a simple chip shot from about thirty-five feet from the green. Was his frustration level increasing because of his golf game, as a result of his quality control problems, or a combination of both? I found out soon enough. What he said next didn't apply in any way to our quality control conversation, but focused on the muffed shot he just made, or didn't make. I didn't realize he possessed the literary skill of making a lengthy compound sentence by using only four-letter words.

When the quality control people presented their numbers to corporate, they were in some cases, as much as forty-five percentage points lower than what Harley calculated and submitted. How could that be? A percentage point here or there could be something as simple as a rounding error, but a forty-five point spread? Something was definitely wrong, but what? I obviously didn't have any answers for Harley, but I did figure out by the third hole why he was confiding in me. Harley knew that the corporate Director of Quality Control and I were relatively good friends and shared several mutual areas of interest. He also knew that I worked with the Director of Quality Control in developing and planning some of the parameters for the corporation's new customer service initiative, the initiative that was causing Harley problems. And a third reason, even though Harley didn't come right out and

Personal Values

say it, was he and Kirt Benson, the Corporate Director of Quality Control didn't seem to get along very well.

Neither Harley nor I needed to worry about playing "customer golf" that day, nor any other day for that matter. Knowing there are always two sides to every story, I suggested to Harley that I would be glad to mention to Kirt, the next time we were together, that we had had this conversation. I promised I wouldn't mention anything about our day's golfing prowess. Maybe I could see if Kirt had any thoughts or ideas about why Harley's numbers differed so much from those Kirt and his quality people had.

It was about a week later when I happened to meet with Kirt to review a related customer service quality proposal he developed and planned to submit for corporate funding. He also wanted to hire a few more people to handle the recent acquisition made by the company. His present staff was already working very thin. Kirt is a very intense individual with a genuine passion for quality and doing what's best for the organization. Many people didn't understand his passion for quality. With a background from high-tech operations, he has the unique ability to visualize the application of quality concepts to just about any manufacturing process. Unfortunately, his people skills are a little weak. What Kirt presents as facts or observations, many times comes across as accusations and hostile criticisms. Even his everyday conversation skills, and his ability at trying to tell jokes, can be misread as "attack" mode. With earmuffs and verbal filtration equipment in hand (mine), Kirt and I got together.

What an interesting meeting it turned out to be! It reminded me of a Sociology 101 demonstration back in college where two subjects were shown the same video, then individually and without hearing the other's response, each observer was asked to describe what he saw. Usually their responses were significantly different, even though they viewed the exact same video under the exact same conditions. Not only were Harley's and Kirt's responses concerning the variances in their production numbers totally different, what they were measuring seemed diametrically opposed as well. If I were a jury member and had to make a decision based on the evidence presented to date by both parties, in the case of *Harley versus Kirt*, my deliberations would have ended quickly in favor of Kirt.

Kirt explained as part of the corporate-wide initiative to focus on customers and customer service, a number of new quality metrics were being requested of manufacturing. The new metrics were intended to address operations from the customer's perspective. The customer interface with the organization, not just from a manufacturing and efficiency viewpoint, but from a service standpoint, was recognized as a potential competitive edge. Kirt explained that when the new guidelines and parameters for the customer service metrics to be measured were forwarded to all the manufacturing managers, they were directed to customize the metrics, if needed, specific to their individual operations and manufacturing systems. Kirt said, "Harley sure seems to have taken that suggestion to heart." Kirt went on to explain that when he and Harley compared numbers for Harley's operation for the first time, they were comparing "...apples to oranges."

As a specific example, Kirt brought up the proposed metric of product being "Shipped on Time." Kirt explained at great length, to the customer, "Shipped on Time" means "did they (the customer) receive it when they were promised or told they would receive the product." Seems at the time the new metric was introduced, Harley was experiencing some equipment and maintenance problems and conveniently "customized" the metric to measure the length of time it took from "order entry to when the product was placed on the truck" for delivery.

Personal Values

"Note, I didn't say received by the customer!" Kirt emphasized. With normal transportation schedules, excluding delays, it could be up to two weeks after the "placed on the truck" date before the customer actually took possession of the product. Harley and Kirt were defining and measuring "Shipped on Time" entirely differently.

In talking with Kirt about the "Shipped Complete" metric, he started to laugh in a way only Kirt can do, between a few cuss words. According to Kirt, when an order could not be completely filled by the promised date, instead of the paperwork being sent back as an "incomplete" order, any product not shipped was reentered into the system under a completely new order number. New order numbers didn't indicate in any way that the order was part of a previous incomplete shipment. With a new order number, the delivery date clock was starting over again. That's convenient! Seems most customers define "Shipped Complete" as receiving everything that was *originally* ordered in one shipment, not split up over several shipments, multiple order numbers, and more than one delivery date.

According to Harley's numbers and measurement approach, the plant was averaging over 99% "Shipped on Time" and "Shipped Complete" scores. When Kirt's people measured the same metrics, the results were closer to the 40 to 50% range for on time and complete, at least from the customers' feedback and point of view.

With regards to the metric for "Service/Warranty Time," the standard guideline suggested by Kirt's Quality Control group was significantly different from what Harley implemented. The guideline was for the plant managers to measure the elapsed time from a customer's original contact with the company (complaints were received via mail, phone, FAX, and e-mail) until the on-site service call was made by the service technicians. A secondary measurement was the time it took the technician, after arriving at the customer's location, to resolve the problem to the customer's satisfaction. Seems Harley was measuring the time from when a complaint was received until it was "scheduled and assigned" to a service technician, not when the technician actually showed up on the customer's steps or when the problem was resolved to the customer's satisfaction. Because of the recent increase in volume of customer complaints, the technicians were making on-site customer visits as much as one month after the date the complaint was received. Assignment of complaints to service technicians was usually completed only hours after the complaint was received from the customers. Measuring hours versus months, no wonder Kirt and Harley had different numbers.

After my meeting with Kirt, I was in no rush to call Harley. I needed some time to think about how I intended to approach the topic with Harley, especially given what Kirt had shown me. Seems my decision on when to talk with Harley was already made for me. Somehow, Harley heard through the grapevine that Kirt and I were together. I'm always amazed at how quickly some information seems to spread around here. Harley called me to find out how things went with Kirt. I was tempted to tell him to call Kirt directly, but thought the better of that approach. I'm also sure Harley picked up on the sudden change in my voice after I realized who was on the other end of the phone. It turns out the call wasn't as difficult as I thought it would be.

I explained to Harley what he was measuring compared to what Kirt's people were looking at seemed to be measurements of totally different metrics. At this point in the conversation Harley didn't disagree, argue, or provide any excuses. In fact, he readily agreed the two sides were measuring totally different things, even though he didn't tell me that during the

Personal Values

round of golf. Harley is not one to try to deceive anyone, but I did feel somewhat set up or used. As we talked, I asked him why he completely altered the measurements he was having his people make, compared to the original guidelines proposed by Quality Control. Equally important was the case of the "Shipped on Time" and "Shipped Complete," metrics and why he'd gone so far as to change well established major internal systems and processes.

The answer I got was quite simple and made perfect sense to Harley. Harley's and his employees' quarterly incentives were directly tied to their achieving 95% or better on the plant's goals and objectives as determined by "corporate." Obviously, Harley found a simple way to inflate his numbers as close to 100% as possible.

I'll lay odds that in the long run Harley's approach will lead him down a path he definitely doesn't want to go. With the increased customer complaints iceberg visible on the near horizon, I'm not sure I care to see the size of the rest of the iceberg, especially the part that's still under water. Harley's incentive checks might be great now, but if his customer complaints continue to rise and orders continue to diminish, I can only guess what those incentive checks will look like in a few years, or even months.

I wonder if Harley ever had a dream of going to Disneyland...

By the way, today Popsicles cost more than six cents each...

Chapter VIII

Taking Credit for Another Person's Work

> *Indeed the Idols I have loved so long*
> *Have done my credit in the World much wrong:*
> *Have drown'd my Glory in a Shallow Cup*
> *And sold my Reputation for a Song*
> Fitzgerald 1809-1883

While I was diligently working early one Tuesday morning, my phone rang at approximately 7:15, just as I was about to go to the employee kitchen and fix my second cup of hot tea for the morning. Would you believe I've never drunk a cup of coffee, cumulative, in my life? Being a bona fide card-carrying member of AARP would suggest it's been a long time. Don't get me wrong about coffee. I love the smell of fresh coffee brewing, but have never acquired a taste for the beverage.

"Good morning, Bryan, this is Bob. How are you this fine morning?" My first thought was "Bob who?" The voice didn't sound familiar, and even if it did, there were several Bobs I know who could have sounded like this particular voice, especially over the phone. I was still new with the company, so my ability to recognize voices and place them with names and faces was being challenged entirely too early this morning.

I responded with a cheerful "Fine. And how are you this beautiful day?" not wanting to ask that most embarrassing two word question. You know the one! "Bob who?" Fortunately, Bob immediately started talking about wanting to set up an appointment at my earliest convenience to discuss a marketing idea he had. The word "marketing" gave me the answer to the "Bob who?" dilemma. Finally, even though it was only seconds into the phone call, I knew who I was speaking to! I could now concentrate on the content of the conversation instead of only the sound of the voice.

Bob continued, "What I'd like to do is bounce this new idea I have off you and see if you might have any suggestions for improving it and hopefully even implementing it. Also, Bryan, I would appreciate the opportunity to officially meet our newest "corporate" manager." Bob placed an obvious emphasis on the word "corporate." Having been with the company for only about a month or so, I wasn't sure what this gesture of goodwill was all about, considering Bob was responsible for the entire corporation's marketing functions. A man of his vast experience wouldn't need to ask me, the newest member of the "corporate" staff, about his area of expertise. The whole conversation started to sound like there was an ulterior motive, but I quickly let that thought slide. I had no reason to question Bob's integrity, I hardly knew the guy.

With a few gray hairs on my head, I'm astute enough to recognize that the term "earliest convenience" is *corporatese*, similar to legalese, for "as soon as possible" or more bluntly, "NOW!" I did have a phone appointment scheduled for 7:30, so I suggested we get together at 8:00 or as soon as I completed my call. "That would be great," Bob replied.

Even before we hung up, my mind started recollecting discussions I'd had with others in the office. You know, the normal chitchat you experience when you're being introduced to everyone in the office, usually all on the same day. Can't really say I remembered all of their names after one encounter, but I guess that's part of the *rite of passage* new employees are required to endure. All the shaking of hands and back-slapping that day probably provided me with enough experience to put on a good public showing should I ever decide to run for political office. My wife says I shouldn't consider running for political office, she says I'm too honest!

Newly introduced colleagues would usually ask if I'd met everyone yet, obviously making a mental check on where they stood on the new introductions pecking order. I would politely answer with something simple, but noncommittal, like, "I'm not sure, but it feels like I've met most everyone." The uneasiness and discomfort of first introductions would usually be prolonged, as they would ask if I'd met so-and-so, or someone they suspected would be important to my long-term career. I would usually respond affirmatively or negatively, whatever the case, but never in an undecided manner. If I had to answer no, I always felt obligated to mention a few names of those I did remember meeting. I guess responding with a name of someone I had met helped prevent the blank stare and questioning silence of the questioner to any "no" response. Because I'm an avid student of communications, and particularly non-verbal communications, there seemed to be consistency in the response behaviors among those I spoke with, especially when particular names were mentioned. For some names, the response was a smile or nod of approval. Other names, evoked obvious frowns or sarcastic tightening of their facial muscles. Sometimes they'd look up toward the ceiling as if a ceiling tile were about to fall. In Bob's case, the consistent response was, well, how should I say it, no response at all. Actually, nobody ever really said anything to me about

Personal Values

Bob, which was fine with me. My personal philosophy is to try to make my own "unbiased" judgments about another individual. Hearing another person's opinions slants my biases even more.

My 7:30 call took a little longer than I'd expected, so my arrival time at Bob's office turned out to be about 8:09. I found his office by reading all the engraved plastic nameplates on my way to the general vicinity of his office. Ah yes, here it is, the "Robert 'Bob' Spencer" office. As I looked into the office, Bob was staring quite intently at his computer monitor. He was seated and facing away from the entry where I was standing. His view out the window revealed another one of those wonderful courtyards scattered strategically throughout our office complex. "Good morning Bob," I said in a voice that hopefully wouldn't startle someone who seemed so intent on what he was doing. Bob quickly spun around on his chair, which, by the way, looked brand new, stood up and firmly shook my hand as he graciously offered me a chair positioned in front of his desk. I wondered if maybe his chair might have been in my office just prior to my arrival… No, probably not. My first instinct and reaction when I go someplace unfamiliar, like another colleague's office, is to check out the surroundings. So I started to scan Bob's office, not only curious to see what was there, but possibly to pick up on any leads I might be able to use to break the ice and find common grounds to establish some rapport and a business relationship. You know what I'm talking about, things like pictures, books, mementos, or anything else that might be a conversation starter. You can tell a lot about someone just by observing their office.

It's amazing how fast the eyes and brain coordinate together to identify and register, for future use, various characteristics within the surrounding environment. Two books, both of which I'd already read, were strategically positioned on top of a side credenza. Both books were recently on the *Business*

Week magazine's non-fiction top seller list. The framed picture on the wall above the credenza was poorly matted, but "corporate" none the less. There was a blue lava lamp among a number of other articles which appeared to be mementos from various business meetings or training seminars. Bob's desk had nothing on it except for a writing tablet with the company logo printed in the top margin and a matching company pen that had the distinct look of a new promotional item. Bob appeared to be very proper and well groomed, wearing a white shirt and coordinated tie. Not quite what you'd see modeled in a Sear's catalog, but not far off.

In an effort to break the ice, establish some level of rapport, and find a possible common ground to start from, I asked Bob what he thought of the book entitled *Market Driven Management*, one of the two books carefully positioned on his credenza. With a little hesitation and two false starts on the first sentence out of his mouth, he indicated it was a very good book. What better way to find some common ground with a new colleague, right? So I proceeded to mention some of the topics I personally found interesting in the book, you know just to start that co-worker bonding process, similar to male bonding that happens while playing sports. Bob hesitated again and then said he'd just recently purchased the book from Amazon.com and up to this point only had the opportunity to quickly skim through it. He anticipated reading it later, emphasizing it was next on his "books to read" list.

Okay, do I try again and mention my interest in the second book sitting on the credenza or should I consider another tactic unrelated to the books? My dilemma was quickly resolved as Bob inquired how my relocation and settling into the new home was going. Relocation at this time was not really a good topic, at least from my perspective. The name Bruno is synonymous with "bad" relocation for me. Without being very specific, I indicated everything was progressing as well as could be expected under the circumstances. I then made some small talk about boxes that weren't opened from a previous move, which had occurred several years before this one. The discussion was similar to the way grad students like to sit around and compare how broke they are, or how hypochondriacs tend to compete with each other about whose medical problems are worse. In similar manner, people who have had to relocate several times compare how many unopened moving boxes they still have from previous moves. Wouldn't you know it, Bob had several stories of his own, even though he and his wife have lived in the same house for the last sixteen years.

I have to compliment Bob for doing his homework! He obviously got a copy of my resume or reviewed my recent employment application, because he was more than familiar with my background and experience. For a moment I wondered what implications the federal Privacy in Employment Act had in this situation, especially because I don't report to Bob, nor are we even under the same executive VP. Oh well, we obviously had more important things to discuss right now than how he gets his information.

Fortunately Bob shifted gears and indicated he was interested in exploring an idea for a project proposal on implementing several cultural changes within his marketing department. The reason we got together in the first place. He wanted to try to change the department's thinking from being traditionally "production driven" to being more "market driven," or as he borrowed the words from the literature, "customer driven." Wow, did he ever hit a nerve for me, and a good one at that! In my background, the topic of "market driven" or "customer driven" companies has been an interest and personal passion for many years. What an opportunity! Now I could share my passion with someone who actually wanted to try to initiate organizational change (another buzzword) within his own department. Just what I wanted, especially with a new employer, an opportunity to participate directly in the project planning process and then be able to influence its implementation. This was definitely going to be better than reading about case studies in the *Harvard Business Review*. I couldn't help but wonder silently to myself if I had unknowingly run across a kindred spirit who had a passion similar to mine?

I'm sure my voice went up two octaves and doubled in speed from my anticipated excitement. Only being with the company for such a short period of time and now this! Here it was, an opportunity to participate in a project that was close to my heart... I could almost feel another adrenaline high coming on. Bob threw around a few more buzzwords on "customer and market driven" organizations, convincing me right there on the spot he was well read and very passionate about the topic. I asked him if he had as yet committed any of his thoughts on the project to paper and if he would be so kind as to share them with me during our conversation. A crestfallen look came across his face as he apologized for having left his project folder at home in his briefcase. But he'd gladly try, because of my obvious enthusiasm, to recall and recreate the general outline of his proposal and writings from memory. As our conversation continued, Bob periodically would scribble down a few words on the company logo tablet in front of him. I never really was able to see exactly what he wrote on that tablet, but it didn't matter to me at the time. In a day or so, he would probably share with me the extensive notes he had at home.

Time flew by and before we knew it, Bob's secretary gently knocked on the open door and reminded him of an eleven o'clock appointment. His visitors had just arrived and were waiting in the main lobby. The secretary's knock on the door, as soft as it was, startled both of us. Eleven o'clock already? As if in disbelief, Bob and I simultaneously glanced at our watches just to verify the time. Sure enough. It was approximately 11:13, at least according to my watch. Where did the morning go? The secretary's knock on the door was also a very welcome gesture. We both were overdue for a "bio-break," the two cups of tea from earlier this morning were finally making their rounds.

With a bit of theatrical exaggeration blended in, we both acted startled by the knock and amazed about the time. Bob flattered me with some admiration about the depth and breadth of knowledge I had about customer service and the concepts of "market driven organizations." I assured him I was only repeating what I'd read in the book sitting on his credenza. As he was quickly attempting to straighten up the top of his desk in preparation for his eleven o'clock appointment by repositioning his tablet and pen, he asked if I would be kind enough to write up, in his words, "a short summary" of our morning's discussion. He also encouraged me to feel free to expand on our dialogue as he managed to slip in the suggestion to utilize any project proposal format I desired. He added he would bring in his notes from home, if he remembered.

Out of my mouth, without even realizing it, flew the response, "Oh sure! Why not! I remember using the old *MLA Style Sheet* from when I did my dissertation so many years ago. I should be able to recall some of the basic rules for project proposal writing."

As a parting gesture, we shook hands as we both muttered, at exactly the same time, something about having enjoyed the morning together. "You know, that Bob sure seems like a real nice guy," I thought to myself as I walked out of his office and navigated my way back toward mine. There was only one thing that seemed to bother me though… Why would anyone his age, which was close to mine, want a blue lava lamp in his "corporate" office? In no other way did he give me the impression he possessed any other latent 1960s baggage.

After lunch, Bob unexpectedly stopped by my office to thank me again for my time earlier in the morning and for the opportunity to get to know each other better. You know, this Bob guy really seems pretty nice, not to mention we hit it off so well and so quickly. As he departed my office, I thought to myself (but, of course, who else could I possibly "think" to), "I'm really looking forward to working with him on this project." I told Bob, as he was headed down the hall, "I'll try to get something together by the end of the week."

He turned around and said, "The first of *next* week would be fine because I'm going to be traveling on business for the rest of this week." Lucky no one was approaching him from down the hall, because by this time Bob was walking backwards as he finished his sentence.

Being a bit compulsive (while my wife is convinced that it's more like anal-retentive) I immediately committed my thoughts to paper and incorporated some of the buzzwords and phrases Bob repeatedly used during our meeting. For whatever reason, I remember a former high school teacher once said something about using other people's exact words. If you use other people's words, almost like flattery, it makes them feel you're truly interested in them and had listened to what they had to say. Because of other work priorities at the office, I spent the next three evenings at home hovering over my laptop, pulling the proposal together. Notice I said "proposal" instead of a summary report. With a topic so near and dear to my heart, along with the subliminal need to gain acceptance from my new colleague, I ended up spending a total of eighteen hours and twenty-three minutes composing a full-blown proposal. The review committee for the National Endowment for the Arts, or any other philanthropic organization's review board would have been impressed with my work. Could you imagine, a thirty-two-page color enhanced proposal, which I even bound with a transparent cover in a Velo-Binder system. I was proud of this masterpiece. My dissertation didn't even come close to the level of eye appeal this document had. Keep in mind my dissertation was done back in the 70s on a manual Underwood typewriter – technology sure makes a difference!

Bob and I didn't have a specific time set aside to get together. We would schedule an appointment after he returned from his business trip. So in the meantime, I kept the proposal on the top right hand corner of my desk. This was too fine a document merely to send to him through inter-office mail. A personal presentation was more appropriate. I sure was impressed with my work, subliminally hoping any visitors coming into my office might see it and comment. No one ever did though.

On Tuesday of the following week, Bob stopped by my office to inquire how the "summary report" was coming along. He also apologized about not providing me his notes from home. Proudly reaching for the document on my desk, I told him I hadn't done the summary report. Instead, I got so deeply involved I ended up with a full-blown, professional quality project proposal. Proudly holding it in my hand, I also indicated I had taken the liberty to include a comprehensive time-line, PERT chart, literature review, and cost estimates, along with appropriate metrics to evaluate the implementation process. "Bob, when would you like to get together to go over the document?" I asked him with an obvious sense of personal pride.

"How about early tomorrow morning? What time do you get in?" Bob asked, as if he got to the office before I did.

"Well let's see," I said as I glanced at my open appointment book, "How about 6:45 here in my office?" When presenting a proposal, it's always better to be on your own home turf. Bob suggested 7:15 instead.

Our 7:15 debrief lasted about two hours. Bob sure seemed intensely interested in every last detail. He would read a sentence, maybe two at the most, and then ask a question or two, continuously soliciting my extensive in-depth details and explanations. Gosh, this was fun! He really was interested in and had a passion for the concepts of "market driven organizations." In my own private way, I was rather satisfied with myself, too. I felt I was the mentor in a two person philosophical discussion. I could tell Bob was impressed and satisfied, no, elated might be a better word, with the document. Near the end of our meeting, I inquired about what Bob thought his implementation timetable might be. He indicated he had several other immediately pressing assignments that were of slightly higher priority, but he anticipated starting on it "as soon as possible." With copies in hand, Bob left my office.

Three weeks quickly passed by and not a single word or other feedback from Bob. That was understandable because we were right at the annual peak of our sales and marketing cycle. In addition, I understood Bob was involved with the field sales teams while concurrently working with a number of our major customers on several marketing projects. How could he have done anything with the proposal? Of the last twenty-one days, Bob had been on the road for fifteen of them.

Every quarter, as part of what's considered by the company an innovative feedback and communications approach, all "corporate" managers are invited, actually required, to attend what's called a "Corporate Managers Forum." Various VPs, selected by the President, would make presentations to the entire group, solicit questions, and, as a panel, provide answers. I later realized, like seasoned politicians, most of their answers were prepared well in advance. All of the VPs, as if seeking approval had a habit of immediately glancing over to the

Personal Values

President after answering a question from the audience to see his reaction(s). Still, not withstanding the group dynamics, the concept of such a meeting sounded great to me. My previous employer never did such a thing. Most executives at my previous employer went to great pains to avoid employees as much as possible well as the rest of the management team. What a great communications tool! This would be the first quarterly forum I would be attending since joining the company. In the back of my mind, I wondered if I could remember the names of all those "corporate" managers I've met since starting here several months ago.

For me, the meeting was very informative and provided a wonderful forum for dialogue and interaction among all the VPs and managers. Some of the vice presidents could benefit from a course in platform and speaking skills, but overall I was quite impressed with the process. This meeting was especially intriguing because near the end of the session, the President was scheduled to address the group and reportedly wanted to share a special accomplishment recently brought to his attention. After making a few introductory statements, the President asked Bob Spencer to share his plans to implement a major organizational change project planned for the marketing department. The project was a first step in the vision of the corporation becoming more "market and customer driven."

"WOW!" I thought to myself. The work Bob and I did was now going to be used as a prototype and foundation for the rest of the organization. I can't wait to hear what Bob has to say.

After the meeting, I walked back to my office with a *different* kind of appreciation for Bob Spencer. He proudly passed out copies of the entire proposal to everyone in the quarterly forum, reviewed the development of the concepts, and finished with the implementation steps. He even fielded a number of questions. As the participants were filing out of the room, comments like "what a change agent" and "he's surely a leading edge innovator for the company" floated through the corridors.

The proposal Bob distributed during the quarterly forum to all the other VPs and "corporate" managers was an exact copy of the document I had so willingly developed. Not a single word was changed or edited from my original proposal except for one, and that change was on the cover sheet. That one change was a substitution of the name "Bob Spencer" in the place of "Bryan Matthews." The name Bryan Matthews was nowhere to be found on the proposal. Did I mention my name was *never* even mentioned during Bob's presentation to the "Corporate Managers Forum?"

I find it rather interesting but sad, and maybe it's a survival instinct on my part, but anytime I now forward anything to Bob Spencer, there's a long circulation list of individuals who receive copies of the correspondence.

Did I mention that Bob has never made direct eye contact with me ever since…?

Chapter IX

Team Player

> *Government and co-operation are in all things the laws of life; anarchy and competition the laws of death.*
> *Ruskin 1819-1900*

Even though many of us didn't realize it at the time, our high school years provided numerous opportunities to explore not only the world around us, but also that world *within* each of us. That world within each of us is what makes everyone unique and identifies who we are as individuals. The academics in the classroom provided the facts and theories, while the extra-curricular and out of school activities provided the practical laboratory where the experimentation and application of those theories took place. The realities of the socialization process and the application of classroom theory to real life combined to create all those meaningful and long-term memories permanently etched into our minds. I can remember a number of significant events that occurred during those high school years that have been imbedded and preserved in my memory forever. Just like you, I can recall many of those significant episodes as clearly today as when they actually happened way back in the early sixties. Every minute detail is as vivid, and probably a little more enhanced and enriched over the years, as if it happened only moments ago. Other than one or two memorable classroom experiences, most of the more significant learning experiences took place outside the classroom or at extra-curricular activities and events.

The high school I attended was quite large compared to most. When I say large, I mean large. There were almost one thousand one hundred students just in my senior class! To say we were a close-knit and intimate graduating class would be a bit of an exaggeration. On the other hand, what we lacked in intimacy was more than made up for in opportunities. Because of the size of the school district, there seemed to be more resources available for opportunities and activities that might not have been available or cost effective at a smaller school. Most students could find at least one interesting activity to participate in. The list went from organized varsity sports (I think there were even several levels of junior varsity teams for every sport), theatre, student government, Future Farmers of America, to the Square Dance Caller's Club, and anything in between. The opportunity was there for any student to find his niche to excel, no matter what his talents or interests. Like most high school students, I found sports, school sponsored extra-curricular activities, and out-of-school activities more important at the time than academics. Not that grades weren't important to me, because they were. With above average grades, I was a member of National Honor Society, participated in student government, National Thespian Society (no we were not a group promoting alternative lifestyles), German club, our church youth groups, and I was a member of the varsity swimming team for three years. Soccer wasn't a popular sport at the time, at least in Western Pennsylvania.

I'm convinced every boy in junior and senior high school had visions of becoming a great All-American athlete, and so did I. Maybe that vision wasn't always openly expressed, but it was there, if only as a fantasy. Football is almost a religion in Western Pennsylvania and the tri-state area. The dream of becoming a high school football star carried with it benefits only a teenage boy can imagine. Things like the fame associated with scoring a touchdown, popularity, college scholarships, dates, and more dates every weekend. All right I'm getting a little carried away, but I did say it was a dream, didn't I?

One major lesson in life's realities occurred when I "thought" I wanted to try out for the high school varsity football team. That "thought" quickly vanished when reality struck, and I realized the pool of potentially *great* players the coaching team had to pick from was astronomical. With one thousand plus students comprising each of the sophomore, junior, and senior classes, it was relatively easy for the football coaching staff to field a good team. With approximately one thousand five hundred boys in tenth, eleventh, and twelfth grades in our high school at the time, and approximately three hundred fifty of them trying out for the team, I knew mathematical probability was against me. Most of the boys, and maybe I should call them men, who were trying out for the football team grew up on local farms. Physically, they seemed to have matured a lot faster than the rest of us. It was very unlikely my weighing in at mere one hundred eighty pounds would qualify me for the front line, or any other position for that matter. A one hundred eighty pound high school boy may sound big, but let's put it into perspective. One year the average weight of the players on the front line was two hundred forty-three pounds. The running backs were agile and fast. In fact, the football team, during my senior year, included six seniors, five juniors, and five sophomores who eventually played professional football. I can't begin to count the number of players who received college football scholarships. Did I really have a chance to make the team, let alone play? Another motivating factor in deciding not to play football was my fear of injury and a very low tolerance for pain, any kind of pain. When I look back and replay some of those memorable high school football championship games I attended as a spectator, I still wonder to this day if there's something in "farm" water that made those country boys so big and strong. During all three years I attended high school, the football team went to the state championships.

Swimming! Now that was my sport, even before I knew I wanted it to be. During a swimming class way back in junior high school, the physical education instructor made that decision for me. He came up to me after swimming the required laps he always made everyone do before the end of each class. He called them "cool down" laps, while most of the class considered them "torture" laps. The tactic was similar to running full speed around the softball field several times after a game. I always thought medical experts said you should do "cool down" laps instead. In the way only a junior high school physical education teacher knows how to do, he looked me straight in the eyes and gruffly announced, not asked, that I would be trying out for the senior high school varsity swimming team the following year. It wasn't a suggestion or even a question, but what seemed like a major proclamation. He made sure, quite intentionally I'm convinced, that everyone in class and within a two-mile radius, heard loud and clear. After his announcement, there was no conceivable way I wouldn't try out for the swimming team. He managed, in one gruff sentence, to establish such peer pressure from my classmates I had no other options. The peer pressure was more in my own mind than from my class mates, but it was still there. During those few seconds, while I shivered from being wet, he determined my next three years' worth of high school varsity sports. If I tried to resist, I was certain that within those three years of high school some kind of embarrassing retaliation would be directed against me. Possibly something as serious as an announcement, as I walked on stage to receive my diploma at graduation, that I didn't try out for the swimming team. Or even worse, the senior yearbook photographer would intentionally make sure he took an "ugly" picture of me for inclusion in a special "losers" section of the yearbook. Could there be any worse fate? Major humiliation during your teenage years is having an ugly senior picture printed in your high school yearbook. Junior pictures are expected to look bad, but not senior pictures. I feared if I didn't try out for the swimming team, the editors of the high school yearbook would put a nasty caption under my picture stating something to the effect that I had no school spirit. For a high school student, such a fate could mark you for the rest of your life. Have you looked at your high school yearbook lately?

The next year, tryouts for the high school swimming team proved very rewarding. My odds of making the varsity team were good, in fact, thirteen out of the fifteen guys trying out for the team made it, and the other two were selected as official equipment managers or timekeepers. Now, tell me, other than a stopwatch and a clipboard, how much equipment was really needed by a swimming team? As a varsity athlete, walking the halls between classes was like walking on air. Letter sweaters drew attention and admiration from the girls and all the other non-jocks. I was selected by the coach to participate in the medley relay and also compete in an individual event. Because of the limited size of the team, almost all of us had to compete in two events. My individual event was the one hundred-yard backstroke, and in addition I led off the fifty-yard backstroke leg of the medley relay team.

After everyone, and I do mean everyone who tried out for the team, was selected as part of the traveling varsity squad, our work began. Practice was every day, Monday through Friday, from 3:30 till approximately 6:00 each afternoon, and from 8:00 till approximately 11:00 on Saturday mornings. That was over fifteen hours a week of practice in the water, in addition to the weight training a majority of us did early in the morning before school started and during study halls. You see, being a varsity athlete had its privileges, like being able to go to the gym and supposedly working out during study hall periods. It was a lot more appealing than sitting in the cafeteria for fifty-five minutes pretending to study. Peeking through the door cracks at the girl's physical education class was an added bonus of that perk. Back then, we thought we were so macho.

The swimming meets didn't quite carry the same prestige nor attract the large crowds football did. No cheerleaders, no band playing the school song or alma mater, no pre-meet pep rallies with bon fires, but for some reason that didn't matter. We were lucky if we averaged even twenty-five spectators at each home, or away, swimming meet. The spectators were usually comprised of several dedicated parents, girlfriends of those swimmers who could persuade or bribe them to show up, and one nerdy math student who literally loved playing with a stop watch and compiling insignificant sports statistics for the school newspaper.

Probably by a rare chance of luck, dedication, and maybe a little hard work, the team actually did quite well two years in a row. We made it to state finals for both my junior and senior years! Talk about a major shock. How would you like to go to the state finals and have to perform in front of a *real* roaring crowd for the first time? We were nearly overcome by tension and nervousness to see nearly five hundred anxious spectators in the stands! No matter whether it was a home or away meet, we were all conditioned to expect our usual twenty to twenty-five spectators filling the stands, all of whom we personally knew. What's so interesting when I reflect back on the dynamics of the team, is how we all worked together and supported each other's accomplishments. Other than in the relay races, swimming is basically an individual sport contributing to the entire team's success. For a couple of years, we had a unique group of swimmers who focused on a single team goal, a coaching staff that believed in us, and a dedicated and supportive, even though small in numbers, following. For whatever the reasons, there was little to no "grandstanding" by any of the swimmers, even though a few individuals had a legitimate right to do so, based on their swimming performance. Our team broke several school and pool records, many of which stood for years. Several of the swimmers, and I must modestly say myself included, ended up ranked in the top five in the state. The sense of teamwork and the way we all pulled together as a unified group was an experience that has stayed with me ever since. Maybe it was the coach. Maybe it was the alignment of the planets. Maybe it was the hormone imbalance boys experience around that age. But whatever it was, it worked!

None of us ever made the draft into professional swimming or diving, or the Olympics for that matter, but most of the fully-paid swimming scholarships to attend college were well deserved and appreciated.

Richard Bronawitz sent me an e-mail asking if I would be willing to work with him on a project team that was going to do a feasibility study on the implementation of an enterprise-wide customer service system for the corporation. Now that's something I thought needed not only to be studied within our company, but launched in some manner or fashion as soon as possible. Such an enterprise-wide system had the potential of inter-linking all aspects of the company with each other in a coordinated effort to better serve customers. Added benefits to the company included reduced costs, better and more efficient communications, streamlined production efficiencies, reduced lead times, and ultimately the most important outcome, the development and retention of a satisfied and loyal customer

Personal Values

base. Instead of responding to Richard electronically, I chose to give him a phone call. In my mind, e-mail is very cold and impersonal, but with a phone call I could ask Richard a few more logistical questions along with suggesting several other individuals I hoped could also be part of the project team.

Richard is a very personable individual person with the fortitude and drive to see a project through to its logical end. His background on enterprise systems was quite limited, but he did have the project management skills needed to coordinate this team made up of diverse people representing departments that have traditionally avoided or intentionally ignored each other. Throughout the company there's almost a "Hatfields and McCoys" type of mind set between many of the departments. Instead of constant fighting, they needed to be cooperatively striving to work closer together. I'm sure you've seen similar problems surface between sales and manufacturing, customer service and marketing, accounting and warranty servicing, or even senior and front line management.

Richard didn't have many answers to my questions, other than to indicate the first meeting of the project team was scheduled for the following week in the corporate training auditorium. The auditorium was selected because it would be large enough to comfortably seat all those invited. I started to wonder if attendance at this meeting was going to be limited in size to a manageable project team or the equivalent of a rowdy stockholder's meeting. The size of the auditorium, which has one hundred twenty-five seats, was probably an overkill for the eighteen people who did show up, but the bagels, soft drinks, and assortment of cookies more than made up for it. Have you ever noticed how certain, if not most, participants at these types of meetings display primitive behaviors akin to starving refugees suddenly presented with food for the first time! The uncomfortable fold down seats didn't help much either.

The various departmental representation at the meeting was remarkable. Along with several Vice Presidents, the group was made up of "corporate" managers from just about every division and department. As Richard began the meeting, you could feel the genuine interest and intensity in the room, even from those who continued chewing cookies and bagels with their mouths open. The concept and implementation of an enterprise system could have major positive benefits for each and every department within the corporation, not to mention the obvious, and transparent, benefits for the customer. For the most part, customers would never see or interface with the system, but they definitely would be beneficiaries of it. The first meeting progressed very well. Richard proposed a project timeline including specific tasks, persons responsible for each assignment, and deadline dates for completion. He sure seemed to have the ability to organize such a massive undertaking and coordinate the diverse personalities in the room. The final product would be a proposal to be submitted to the Board of Directors for consideration and approval. The funding needed for the project would be high, but the potential returns could be astronomical both in hard and soft dollars. Talk about a definite competitive advantage, especially in our traditional industry. Assignments were made; some were voluntarily accepted while others more reluctantly so. The next meeting was scheduled for the following month, but this time in one of the smaller meeting rooms. I wondered if bagels and cookies would be served, I hope not.

All the participants at the second meeting, only three and a half weeks later, were well prepared. Most of their assignments were completed and it appeared the project enthusiasm level was increasing instead of decreasing. Usually, within our company, by the second meeting of most special project teams, the level of enthusiasm is in a free-fall downward spiral. But for this project, the goals and objectives identified as part of the proposed enterprise system were starting to solidify. The meeting provided the vision and framework for managers to recognize future departmental and division opportunities for success. Everyone appeared to understand the potential benefits of such an innovative system. Some of the participants were even offering solutions and submitting potential alternative outside vendors for consideration. The ideas were flying, and this wasn't even one of those expensive fancy facilitator led "brainstorming" sessions. The suggestions included everything from turnkey solutions to complete internal development of the systems. Richard was a master! In his low-key but commanding way, he managed to refocus the meeting, which was getting out of hand, back to its original agenda, and continued following a formalized project management process. At the first meeting, he had presented a project management model he planned to follow. He quickly placed a transparency of the model on the overhead projector and reminded everyone that we needed to address and successfully complete *all* steps in the model if this project was going to be a success. Skipping even one critical step would invariably lead to problems, frustrations, and possibly even failure down the road. Did Richard ever have the ability to put things into perspective! As if by magic, he regained control of the meeting.

The logistics of implementing any kind of company-wide system are undoubtedly complex. A solution that would optimize the sales process(es) in all probability would not be completely satisfactory for manufacturing, or vice versa. Business and financial priorities, along with the sequencing of any installations, could also lead to problems. Seems everyone wanted to be "on line" first, sort of like being the first in your block to get a satellite dish or a new sport utility vehicle.

With this group, the inevitable started to happen...

The VP for Marketing, who envisions himself as an eloquent speaker, attempted to gain allies to rally around and show support for *his* personal "marketing" agenda. Even though it was obvious to everyone else in the room his persuasion and presentation skills put him in the same category as a television spokesman for the World Wrestling Federation, he focused exclusively on *his* departmental needs at the expense of everyone else. A few days after the meeting we discovered the external consultant he recommended and adamantly supported to head up the project, turned out to be, in his words, his brother-in-law by his first wife. I guess that means it was an "ex" brother-in-law.

The VP for Manufacturing envisioned an enterprise-wide system that had production as the focal point with all other functions supporting it. His PowerPoint graphic turned out to be the equivalent of a pre-schooler's picture of a wagon wheel with manufacturing at the center. Surrounding the manufacturing hub were tiny spokes pointing outward toward all the other departments and support functions. The font used for the word "manufacturing" was about three times bigger than that used for the other "support" departments and functions depicted on the graphic. The "customers" didn't rate enough to get a spoke, nor were they even represented in any way on his picture. He took great pride in stating he doesn't meet with or work directly with any external customers, so there was no need to include them as part of the enterprise system. After looking at his graphic, most everyone I spoke with after the meeting thought it might help if he took a remedial course in how to use PowerPoint. It was also suggested that possibly the VP for Manufacturing might want to find out exactly who purchases and pays for our products. Here's a hint: It's a nine-letter word that starts with a "C" and ends in "S."

Personal Values

The "corporate" Manager for Warranty Services presented page after page of statistics supposedly representing the number of customer contacts his department handled in any given week. He probably assigned one of his administrative assistants to gather and manipulate those numbers in every imaginable permutation for comparison purposes. With all the numbers and statistics he presented, a casual observer might think he was the lead actuary of statistical demographics for the U.S Census Bureau. If the numbers weren't enough to overwhelm and bore everyone in the room, he then proceeded to assign blame for his department's problems on all the other departments and support services that interface with his. If this is an example of how he treats us, his "internal customers," I wonder how he and his staff treat our "external customers?" Let's see, that last word has nine letters, begins with the letter "C" and ends with an "S." Maybe he and the VP for Manufacturing need to get together.

In addition to showing the rest of the group his year-end projections for sales, the VP for Sales employed some of the most outdated and over-used sales tactics in history. Some of them apparently were borrowed from what he claimed was his favorite literary work, and where he learned most of his sales and management skills, "Death of a Salesman." Considering his age and all, he must have had Willie Loman as a mentor in his earlier sales life! Unfortunately, his understanding of an enterprise-wide system was very limited. To him, "Enterprise" was the name of a cruise ship. As one known for finding computers and technology a bit intimidating, he positioned his needs based on a sales contact management model directly out of a 1950s training manual for time and territory management.

The "corporate" Director for Information Services was suffering from visions of technological grandeur. All he could see was the acquisition of hardware and software that would make the engineers at NASA drool. He used more "mega...," "nano...," and "giga..." prefixed words than the writers for "Mork and Mindy" could ever have dreamed of. Being the accommodating type, he stated his department was most anxious to get started on this project. One major dilemma he faced, however, was *his* need to reprioritize all the other "corporate" projects that were creating a backlog in *his* department. Even though he had the largest and most rapidly expanding department in the entire corporation, numbers-wise, he never seemed to have enough *qualified* people. At least that's what he said. He was among several other managers and VPs rumored to be building fiefdoms.

The "corporate" Comptroller employed a modified aristocratic approach to his presentation. He philosophized on the "changing world of work," the need for outstanding leadership, and challenged everyone in the room to reexamine all their old paradigms. From his point of view, "It's our old and outdated paradigms that keep us from being "world class," not an enterprise system." He emphatically stated he personally would do anything and everything to make whatever enterprise system we did choose a success, but with one caveat. The new enterprise system needed to be based on the corporate accounting and financial systems he already had in place. Not to stereotype those bean counters and "corporate" financial types, but it's rumored the last time he opened his wallet a moth was observed flying out.

The VP for Research and Development, who was preoccupied with doodling, didn't say a word during the whole meeting, nor did he give a presentation. On a short memo sent to the project team prior to the meeting, he stated his department would assist in any way they could, period. Now that's the epitome of a committed team player!

Richard was visibly annoyed with the proceedings and how they were transpiring right before our eyes. How was he going to get not only the meeting back on track, but get everyone to recognize and understand the benefits of working as a team and looking at this project from a macro perspective? He did what most project managers would probably do at a moment like this - scheduled another meeting.

As everyone was filing out the door, they started whispering and huddling with their targeted or perceived allies out in the hall, around corners, or on their way to the rest rooms. Richard seemed discouraged, so I paused for a moment to ask if there was anything I could do, under the circumstances, to assist him. It seemed he just needed someone to serve as a sounding board, if just for a moment. The individual motivations and self-centered interests of the VPs had undermined Richard's agenda. Instead of taking me up on my offer, and in a very dejected tone of voice, he said he needed some time to think about how to get the project back on track. He went on to say this meeting reminded him of his senior year in high school when the football team *he* played on lost every game. There was definitely talent on the team, but no one pulled together as a cohesive unit. After several losses, even the coaches seemed to lose interest in working with the players, and by the end of the season, there were more players on the field than there were spectators in the stands. Every player, in his own way, contributed to the demise of that football team. He was getting the same uncomfortable feeling with this project.

As we walked out of the meeting room together, I asked him, "Why didn't you go out for swimming instead?"

Chapter X

Six Degrees of Connectivity

> *O what a tangled web we weave,*
> *When first we practise to deceive!*
> *Scott 1771-1832*

Have you ever heard of, or attempted to test the theory that states we're all connected to each other by no more than six other people? Hopefully I can simply explain the concept without making it more complicated than it really is. The theory's hypothesis states we can each be linked to any random individual or can trace a theoretical contact with *anyone* else through no more than six other people. Let's try it. I, Bryan Matthews grew up in Western Pennsylvania with a friend named Tom (Contact Number One). Tom moved to San Francisco and works with Jean (Contact Number Two), who is the girlfriend of Walter (Contact Number Three). Back in college, Walter was a fraternity brother of Christopher (Contact Number Four) who now lives in Dallas. Christopher's wife Annette (Contact Number Five) is a regional sales manager who calls on Ross (Contact Number Six), your neighbor. You see, we are connected! I'm not sure how valid the theory is if applied internationally. Maybe it needs one or two more contacts.

The major problem with implementing the theory is determining all the possible relationship contacts that already exist for everyone, including yourself, then tracing the appropriate lines between those contacts. I'm sure there is a computer that can actually do the job if it has all the right information, but I doubt anyone soon will attempt it on a comprehensive national basis. Getting an accurate U.S. census every ten years is difficult enough. Could you imagine the number of dead ends we might run into before we found the connections that worked? I'm not here to prove or disprove the Six-Degrees of Connectivity Theory, but I learned at an early age it seems to be true. I'm also confident, in most cases, the number of connections is a lot less than six degrees.

Throughout elementary, junior high, and senior high school, all, and I do mean all, my friends and I were convinced our parents, and especially our mothers, had eyes in the backs of their heads, in addition to the two up front. No matter what we thought we were doing, or might be attempting to get away with, it seems our mothers, and don't leave out the dads, always knew what was up even before we got home on any particular day. Our parents always knew exactly what devilment we were into, whether it was in school related activities, outside activities, or even when we were just "hanging around" doing nothing. In certain circumstances, and without us knowing it at the time, our mothers and fathers mysteriously gathered and filed away embarrassing and potentially incriminating information in a secret, but permanent, database in their brains. Over the years, diplomatically in their approach, they would subtly let us know when we least expected it, that they knew even our deepest secrets. Many of those secrets we believed had been hidden forever. In some cases, it took several years or even decades before they revealed the secrets they knew. Keep in mind I'm talking about the time before databases were even conceived in an engineer's wildest dream.

Young children experience a number of formal and informal "rites of passage" during their maturation process. Some of the formal ones include things like high school graduation, obtaining a driver's license, election into student government, taking oaths of office for various organizations, receiving awards or honors, or suffering through your first "real" date. There are also a number of informal rites of passage most kids experience that don't hold the same level of pomp and circumstance as the formal ones do, but they're just as personally significant, if not more so.

Throughout junior high and senior high school, there were several friends my age who developed a very close bond. At the time we were inseparable companions. But unfortunately after high school graduation, we all went our separate ways in search of our own individual American dream. Even though we don't visit or get together much anymore, if at all, the bond is still there and I'm sure will continue well into our *senior* years. Every weekend, and when possible in the evenings, we were together. Tom and John were brothers, as were Harry and Alex. We all went to the same church, which meant our parents were also friends. As a small group of five, we were quick to realize not only did we have our own biological parents, but we also had several sets of "adopted" parents. I can assure you, our parents took their "adopted parent" roles quite seriously.

No matter what time of the year it was, our weekend and evening activities together coordinated with the seasons and weather. Summers were spent swimming and boating, autumn was dedicated to playing pickup football, winter meant snow sports and indoor activities, and spring usually included tennis

Personal Values

and anything that would help push the summer season. Because the senior high school had the best athletic facilities in town for football, tennis, basketball, track, and all those other outdoor sports boys that age like to play, we would usually end up at the school grounds. Other kids our age would do the same, so when we were interested in a team sport, we always seemed to have the necessary competition readily available.

The topography of Western Pennsylvania is made up of forested rolling hills. The valleys were perfect protection from cold winter winds while the hilltops provided gentle but cool breezes that were most enjoyable on a late summer's eve. Lying on the ground and staring up at the stars was one of those pastimes we all seemed to enjoy. While gazing at the heavens, our conversations would range from sports and philosophy to the size of the universe, second only to our *fantasies* about girls. We were not all at the same level of interest or maturity when it came to the "girls" topic.

The school and campus sports facilities were located at the top of a large hill overlooking the town. Its location and the view from the school made a great setting to stare off into the distance and daydream during class. The football stadium and other athletic facilities were located on fill ground that came from the excavation and grading when the school buildings were constructed. The back edge of the football stadium and practice facilities dropped immediately down into a valley and provided another beautiful view of the countryside.

I remember the day very well. It was a Sunday afternoon in late September. The chill in the air made for a perfect afternoon to play touch football. The trees were changing into their colorful autumn splendor and would shed their leaves within a few more weeks, but that was of little concern to us. What was of concern to us was practice. Now you probably think I was referring to football. I wasn't. Football was our alibi and the reason given to our parents for getting together. We were going to practice swearing among ourselves. Now that might sound a little odd, but just about every truthful male I've shared or conveyed this story to usually admits he too has done the exact same thing, or at least something very similar. For whatever reason, there was something intriguing about using words that were forbidden for us to freely use anywhere else. Maybe we couldn't use them elsewhere, but if we collectively agreed not to tell anyone, we felt comfortable to use them within the confines of our friendship. We knew the day would eventually come when we grew up that we could use those swear words. But for now, parental pressure made sure we didn't utter such things. The words we used and started practice on were very tame compared to what I hear children and adolescents say today in their casual conversations on the street or most public places. I even hear the words when they're accompanying their parents. Those forbidden words, those "grounded-in-your-room-for-a-week" words, today are common language, heard any weekday evening even on the major television networks during what's considered "family" programming.

As we were walking up the hill towards the football stadium for our practice session, we selected the five or six particular words we would concentrate on that afternoon during our football game. We would analyze, discuss, and sometimes argue about the various connotations of each of the words and then determine in what specific contexts they could or should be used. We even developed what we thought were appropriate practice sentences we might be able to use later in life when we could use such words. First, just to get started, we would each say the word out loud. Then we would choose an imaginary scenario in which to use the word, and determine the appropriate tone, pitch, and speed in which to use it. As one of us individually practiced using the words, the rest of us would listen intently and evaluate if the word came across as intended. We believed in group consensus, and feedback from the others was always welcome. Even during our football games, we would attempt to use the practice words at what we considered the appropriate times, like after being knocked down or when a particular play was in question.

After a long afternoon of playing football and diligently practicing our vocabulary at *every* conceivable opportunity, we would gradually make it back to one of our homes for refreshments. If we were really lucky, an invitation to stay for dinner was extended by Mom Number Two or Three and always eagerly accepted. Did you ever notice that somehow dinner always seemed to taste better at someone else's house, while in turn, my friends felt the same way about eating at our house. This particular afternoon, we started walking towards Harry and Alex's home, mainly because it was the closest to the school, strategically located on the way home for the rest of us, and probably most important was our bouts with thirst were getting to the point of becoming overwhelming. About halfway there, we knew enough to end our four-letter-word practice session. As we seated ourselves on the porch and Mom Number Three brought us some juice and a snack, we continued to boast about our outstanding football plays of the day and tried to decide who deserved to be chosen the "player of the game." After about ten minutes, Mom Number Three joined us on the porch, sat on the swing, which was suspended from the ceiling, and listened to our post-game coach's corner discussion.

In a way only mothers of early teenage boys can do it, Mom Number Three pulled a neatly folded piece of paper and pencil out of her pocket and said she would like to share with us some football terminology she recently learned. Across the top of the piece of paper were our six practice words for the day. Down the left-hand side of the paper were our names. She made a very neat matrix with thirty squares on it. Within each rectangular block were tick marks. Needless to say, she heard *every* "practice" word we used during the afternoon. Since she knew our voices, it appeared she probably had all the tick marks appropriately placed on the matrix. What we didn't realize that afternoon was the weather and wind conditions were perfect for our voices to carry directly down the valley and onto the porch where she was sitting. What a demonstration in acoustics! Who knows how many other neighbors were subjected to our "practice!" Things got very quiet on the porch as she shared her matrix with us. It was so quiet we too could clearly hear the action still going on at the intramural field right next to where we'd been "practicing." We heard the action as if we were still on the sidelines. For the five of us, the rest of what was left of the afternoon, before dispersing and going home, was spent accusing each other of having been too loud on the football field.

When I arrived home that night I realized those proverbial eyes on the back of my mother's head were actually the eyes, and ears in this case, of Mom Number Three. We didn't know about it at the time, but the Six-Degrees of Connectivity Theory was really the One- or Two-Degrees of Connectivity Theory, especially in our small community.

You remember Robert "Bob" Spencer, the VP of Marketing from a little earlier, don't you? Bob was anticipating starting the process of recruiting for a newly created position within his department. Maybe I should back up a little and define what I mean by "starting the process." For Bob, "starting the process," means no written job description, no advertising plan, no timetable, no defined salary ranges, and no organizational chart to define the position's reporting and supervisory relationships. Bob knew that in one of my previous lives I was involved in corporate recruitment and hiring. Remember, as I mentioned in an earlier chapter, he had seen, and perhaps still had a copy of my resume, despite the fact I wasn't even in the marketing department? Somehow, he also learned from another unidentified colleague I had a software program that created job descriptions. The descriptions produced by the software complied with the guidelines of the D.O.T. D.O.T. in this case is short for the Dictionary of Occupational Titles, not the Department of Transportation. I never looked to see if maybe he had eyes in the back of his head.

Even though most casual observers to our working relationship would probably rate it medium- to low-cordial, I agreed to assist him in developing the job description for his new position. I wondered how our relationship could be rated "medium- to low-cordial" considering his working relationship with just about everyone else was "low-cordial to non-existent." After I asked him a number of standard questions anyone would use in the development of a job description, it quickly became obvious to me he was fashioning the position somewhat after my role in the corporation. He even went so far as to set minimum qualifications around my background. I was starting to wonder if he was trying to tell me something?

With help from the software program, I quickly helped Bob finalize the job description and in addition, provided him with some recommendations and suggestions for an advertising, recruitment, and selection process. I even went so far to offer my services in interviewing his final two or three candidates, if he so desired. That way Bob could have input from another "trusted" source external to his department, but familiar with the functions of the new job. He seemed most grateful for the offer and said he would definitely take me up on it. Even though our working relationship was medium- to low-cordial, I felt it was my responsibility and obligation to try as a "corporate" manager to develop it in a more positive direction. On the other hand, I'm also known to be a glutton for punishment and abuse.

It was about two months later when both Bob and I were early for an update meeting on employee benefits. The manager for employee benefits was conducting informational meetings for the management and supervisory personnel on some upcoming changes in the benefits package scheduled to be effective the following January 1st. When I walked into the meeting room, the overhead projector and screen were already aligned. The video player and monitor were positioned for everyone to see. Stacks of what appeared to be handout materials were neatly arranged face down on the front table. In all probability they were intentionally placed face down so no one could casually see the front cover by mistake, before being ceremoniously distributed to the group. As I scanned the rest of the room for signs of life, my eyes were immediately drawn to the center. Right there in the front row of the middle section of the room sat Bob. Not another soul in the room! Now, how do you graciously take a seat somewhere away from Bob and continue to pretend you're busy for another fifteen minutes waiting for the others to gradually trickle in? I didn't even have a pen or tablet to use as a possible diversion. Walking over to the middle of the room, I greeted Bob with a warm handshake while saying something to the effect that I was glad to see him. As usual, he limited his eye contact with me to less than a second, but was cordial none the less. After the greetings and a few false starts at conversation, I thought a good route to pursue till others hopefully joined us in the room, might be to ask about the status of his recruitment efforts over the past several months. I hadn't seen any announcements of a new hire, nor had he taken me up on my offer to interview his final candidates. On the other hand, two months was a relatively short period of time considering the caliber of the person he was looking for, and considering it was based on *my* qualifications.

Bob enthusiastically proceeded to tell me about the progress he was making to date. I felt quite flattered when he indicated the job description and my suggestions were extremely helpful and that the process appeared to be producing positive results. In fact, he told me he anticipated narrowing the candidates down to the top three within a week or two, then doing a third interview with each before making his final decision. Again, I told him my offer still stood. I offered to interview his two or three finalists as he previously indicated he wanted me to do. Maybe things were slowly starting to develop between us, at least as colleagues. As the room started to fill with other managers, I was looking, probably conspicuously, for any excuse to move and change seats. Racing through my mind was the thought (more like a desperate wish) there must be someone I needed to visit or talk with who might be conveniently seated near the back or corners of the room. No such luck! Just then Sarah from the retirement benefits office walked in and sat in the seat next to me. Her manager was giving the presentation today and Sarah was there to critique and provide feedback for her manager on the newly developed presentation. As she nested herself in the chair, she asked if I was saving the seat for anyone else. Since she was already seated before asking the question, and I couldn't think of a different response fast enough, I didn't have much choice but to welcome her and remain seated, with Bob on my other side.

The bottom line message presented, along with brightly colored graphics, by the end of the meeting was that our monthly employee contributions to the benefits package were going up by what seemed to me like a substantial amount on January 1st. No one in the audience seemed to care. Not one question was posed from the audience after the presentation.

Two weeks to the day after the benefits meeting, Terry Johns stopped by my office. What a pleasant surprise! Terry came to the company as part of an acquisition, and after all the dust and smoke settled, he was appointed General Manager for the newly acquired facility. Terry and I go back about seven years, when we were with a previous employer. Terry had been the Assistant General Manager at the time of this most recent acquisition. Now that he was under our corporate umbrella, we joked a while about "never burning bridges" and "what goes around comes around." After joking around for a little, we caught up on the whereabouts of several other mutual friends. Terry was visiting the "corporate" office today in an effort to meet with a number of production managers and the VP of Manufacturing, so his time was tightly scheduled and limited for the rest of the afternoon.

"How about coming over to the house tonight for dinner? You don't need to stay in your motel room when we could share a glass or two of wine together," I suggested. Need I tell you his response?

An extra steak on the grill and another baked potato in the oven didn't challenge the culinary artistry of this chef very much. The Merlot tasted wonderful, but that was probably attributed more to the evening's companionship and conversation than to the wine's palatability or bouquet. "Palatability" and "bouquet," those were two words I recently learned from a VP who fancies himself a wine connoisseur. He regularly uses "connoisseur" and "aficionado" to describe himself! Problem was, he was suffering from visions of grandeur. I'm sure he privately, but religiously, practiced being a wine snob in front of a mirror. I understand it takes years of practice to learn how to hold a wineglass above one's head and natural eye level then look with awe at something in the wine. As someone who enjoys drinking wine, I remember once telling that snobbish VP, "I didn't realize such fancy descriptive words and the mention of a screw top wine bottle go together in the same sentence, or same conversation for that matter." He didn't find very much humor in my comment. At the time, a number of other thoughts raced through my mind but I used my better judgement and kept my mouth shut.

Personal Values

Generally, I don't like to talk business in the evenings, especially at home with friends. For many years I've believed in and tried to live by the philosophy that a person needs to separate his work life from his personal life. Dinner at home with my wife and an old friend falls under the category of personal life. Terry and I did break that rule, though just for a little while, during our conversation midway through the evening. During and after the acquisition, Terry hosted a number of the corporate team members who were part of the due diligence process. He answered many of their questions and served as an ombudsman during the transition. He named some of the "corporate" people he met and made a few interesting, but accurate, editorial comments about a few of them. Terry is usually one who refrains from talking about others or making judgments about them, but the Merlot and our years of trusted friendship probably helped him feel more relaxed. He would mention an individual, state his first impressions about him, then solicit mine to see if we agreed or disagreed. Notice I said "him," because there were no women on the due diligence team. In most cases, our impressions coincided with each other, except for one, the Quality Control Manager, Kirt Benson.

Terry stopped in mid-sentence and said, "Oh yeah, I just remembered. I knew there was something else I wanted to ask you. When I heard it, I couldn't believe my ears. In my discussions with Bob, ah, what's his last name? Spence? Spencer? That's it! Spencer! He indicated he'd been diligently working on filling the Marketing Manager's role for our facility, but was having limited success up to this point. He said he had a "great" candidate for the position, interviewed him, and even made him a great offer, but the candidate for some unknown reason turned it down. He really spoke highly of the candidate, implying this personally selected candidate walked on water, provided the water was frozen. Bob said the candidate was an internal person who he was sure I didn't know, then he said your name, Bryan Matthews."

I almost choked on the sip of wine I was swallowing. Well, maybe it was more like a gulp instead of a sip. No, I didn't spit or spray it all over the room like they do on television or in the movies. A number of simultaneous thoughts raced through my mind in that nanosecond right after Terry said my name. First of all, I never interviewed for any position with Bob. Secondly, Bob is one of those people I would never work for, and I do mean *never*. Third, why would Bob even bring up the topic of the new position with Terry when he obviously hadn't done anything about filling it yet, other than what I provided for him - the job description and process. Fourth, why would he say he had discussed the position with me? A fifth thought also raced through my mind, but I dismissed it rather quickly. Bob did say he had a "great candidate" who "walked on water!"

Terry said he was very surprised when he heard Bob mention my name. He also indicated Bob said the same thing about me to Terry's Assistant General Manager and several others during the due diligence process. Terry said he couldn't believe it when he heard what Bob said, but figured he'd find out soon enough. This evening was obviously the "soon enough."

The next day I made a concerted effort to talk with one of Bob Spencer's direct reports, Matt Larson. Matt, who most logically would be the one responsible for helping Bob in the recruitment and hiring process for the new position was a frequent golf partner of mine. Matt said he knew of no progress made to date or even any action Bob had taken to fill the position. Matt knew I had helped Bob with the job description and made some suggestions, but that was the only activity so far he knew about.

Personal Values

Bob Spencer unexpectedly walked into the men's room just as I was drying my hands with a paper towel. I thought I needed to speak with our corporate purchasing agent because the paper towels had the feel and consistency of steel wool. Cost cutting is appropriate, but there are some limits! In his amiable, but what now seemed to me to be an insincere way, Bob asked, "How are things going in your world Bryan?"

Should I? Why not?

"I'm a little tired today but overall everything's good," I replied. Before Bob could utter another word I continued with, "These late evenings seem to take their toll on me more than they used to. In fact, last night my wife and I enjoyed a wonderful dinner and an evening of conversation with an old friend. Bob, I think you met him during the acquisition due diligence process. He mentioned your name last night. You remember meeting Terry Johns, don't you?" Without giving Bob a chance to respond I continued, "We must have talked well past one o'clock this morning!" Bob seemed a little surprised when I said Terry's name, but still managed to hold his composure.

Bob didn't utter a word as I quickly went out the door. I felt justifiably smug about my restroom performance. Just before I heard the men's room door close behind me, a thought passed through my mind. I wonder if Bob is familiar with the Six Degrees of Connectivity Theory...

Chapter XI

Status

It is impossible, in our condition of Society, not to be sometimes a Snob.
                                    Thackeray 1811-1863

Have you ever looked up the word "status" in the dictionary? We all have our own specific connotations for the word depending upon the context in which it's being used. Webster's Dictionary defines status as *position or rank in relation to others* or *relative rank in a hierarchy of prestige.* Whatever your definition, it seems the concept of "status" is learned at a very early age for some people, learned later in life for others, and for some, the application of the concept of "status" is unimportant. For me, I'm most impressed and drawn to those in the third group, where status and the *hierarchy of prestige* are unimportant. Over the years, I've come to realize there aren't just one or two universal categories of status, but many. Status and what it means or signifies changes over time for each person and the specific situation he might be in at the time.

Personal Values

Every young boy, at least from my experience, dreams of the day when he graduates from a red wagon or pedal car, today it's probably a Big Wheel or something similar, to a two-wheel bicycle. I'm not talking about a small two-wheeler with training wheels, but instead, a "big" bike. There's a sense of independence, or maybe the feeling of growing maturity, as that new two-wheeler provides a feeling of freedom and the opportunity to venture faster and farther than ever before. There's a quickly learned limitation on how far one can venture on a tricycle, wagon, or even a scooter. Whether it was for a milestone birthday or Christmas gift, the "big" bicycle usually marked an important transition from one phase of growing up to another. That transition was but another step in the long road to independence and venturing out on your own, starting, and in most cases continuing, the separation process from the guidance and direct supervision of your parents. Finally, the means and freedom to go! At least it seemed that way in perspective. The same feeling of independence is experienced at various other times throughout life, like when you get your driver's license, your first car or truck, move off to college, or turn old enough to legally walk into a bar and order a drink. The list can go on and on.

I took possession of my first "big" two-wheeler when I was in second grade. In my mind, this was unquestionably a "real" bicycle. It was a monster machine with twenty-six inch wheels, instead of those "little" eighteen or twenty-inch bicycles kids usually get as a transition into the world of "adult" bikes. I didn't receive the bike as a birthday or Christmas gift, but more as an unexpected opportunity and practical business matter. This acquisition was the result of intense negotiations with an older neighbor boy under the guidance of my parents. The negotiations took place when the neighbor decided he didn't want the bike any longer. He had his sights set on another treasure more important to a young man his age. He decided he was too old and mature for the bicycle, but more importantly, he needed to liquidate some personal assets in order to raise capital. Definitely timing! Being in the right place at the right time, I thought. He asked me if I'd like to purchase the bike for a whopping five dollars. For a second grader, that was a lot of money. But on the other hand, for an opportunist like me, what a deal! But who had five dollars! After a visit to the local community bank and talking with the older lady behind the counter, she graciously suggested I start with my parents. She said something about my not having a verifiable credit history and the bike couldn't be used as collateral, whatever that meant. Her guidance paid off. After presenting a well-planned, written proposal to my parents about why I needed the bicycle, along with highlighting the fact that time was of the essence because such fine merchandise would surely go quickly at the asking price or possibly higher, they agreed to help. They would underwrite the finances for the transaction and counsel me during negotiations. I even agreed, in theory of course, to forgo birthday and Christmas presents for the rest of my life if I could only get this bike. I used the same tactics all children use when they want to get their first puppy or any other "first" pet. Years later I found out my parents called the seller's parents, without my knowing, to make sure the bike was legitimately for sale. Surrounded by the neighbor boy's parents and mine, we finally came to an agreement on the terms and conditions of the transaction. The horn, handle bar tassels, and battery operated light, batteries included, came as part of the deal and remained as added accessories already attached to the bicycle. In turn, I agreed to clean and maintain the bike in good operating condition along with operating it in a safe and *reasonable* manner. With a look of anticipation and excitement only a second grader can manage, I glanced at my father as he produced a five dollar bill from his pocket. It went directly from my father's hand to mine, and quickly into the hand of my business associate. My hand was clutching the seat of the bike during this entire process. I heard something about possession being fifty percent of ownership, so I kept my hand on the merchandise during the whole transaction. With the deal finally completed, both parties left with a satisfied "Win/Win" feeling.

I proudly pushed the bike across the lawn toward our home with visions of entering and winning the next *"Tour de France."* I could envision how proud my parents would be as I wore the victor's traditional Yellow Jersey and held the trophy high. Worldwide television would be covering the victory!

Upon arrival home, it was time to inspect the bike and learn all about its operation and maintenance, similar to reading the owner's manual but without the manual. The owner's manual wasn't part of the deal because there wasn't one. But from my point of view, inspecting the bike from front tire to rear fender reflector seemed appropriate. What a bike! Twenty-six inch wheels! Solid steel tubular frame, which alone my father estimated weighed a minimum of fifty pounds! Contoured saddle for easy riding! One-speed forward gear with brakes applied by reversing the direction of the foot pedal! The single switch adjustable headlight was perfect for night riding provided there was a real bright moon overhead or you were riding in a lighted area. The horn made a sound that was music to my ears, but drove my parents crazy. There was one problem, but I guess it fell under the "buyer beware" laws. After counting the number of strands in the handle bar tassels, the left handle bar tassel had one less strand than the right one. Even though it might be tough, I finally decided I could live with that one flaw. In all probability, no one would ever notice the missing strand except me.

After thoroughly and lovingly washing and waxing the wheels, handlebars and fenders, it was time to take it out for the maiden voyage. Having never ridden a twenty-six inch bike before, especially one with the "boys" bar in the middle, I was filled with anticipation and a bit of anxiety. Dad helped steady the bike next to the porch steps as I managed to climb aboard. Just like at the rodeo, I was ready for the gate to open. Even though my toes couldn't touch the pedals when they were in the bottom position, and after a few spills before moving two feet, which I called false starts, a successful trip was underway down the concrete driveway. At the end of the driveway, instead of using the pedal brake, or spragging my feet, to slow down for the turn and return trip back toward the house, panic struck and the bike and I unceremoniously ended up in the ditch. My pride suffered more pain than my body. After a less than graceful landing in the ditch, I started to wonder if the humiliation of owning a "girls" bike would be less painful than what I'd just experienced. With big tears rolling down my cheeks, I pushed the bike back to the house in anticipation of a better day tomorrow. Falling asleep that night was difficult. Not because of the injuries sustained in the accident, but from worrying if I might be able to master riding it the next day without getting injured again! My mind was also practicing the order in which I would describe the fine features and accessories of the bike as I proudly boasted about my newly acquired wheels to my friends at school.

Lunch break couldn't come soon enough that day, but when it did, my heart was pounding and I couldn't seem to talk fast enough. I described all the fine features and precision engineering of my new bike. As a close knit group of potential Tour de France competitors, we started planning our next bike outing, even though we never had a first bike outing, in anticipation of eventually making a cross-country trip.

Just about the time our table was reveling in our anticipated bicycle feats of fame and notoriety, another student from the lunch table next to ours, joined us and stood at the head of our table. In no uncertain terms, James Cortney Montgomery III, announced to everyone at our table he "accidentally on purpose" (my words) overheard our excited conversation and concluded we knew absolutely nothing about bicycle touring like he did. In no uncertain terms he made it clear to us that *his* "new bike" with ten speeds, aluma-lite frame, ergonomically designed seat and handlebars, automatic derailleur, and torsion bar suspension was the only kind of bike he would ever consider riding. We all probably thought of something else he could put his butt on besides his fancy bike. Definitely, our bikes were far inferior to his, at least in his eyes. After a few forceful "Oh yeahs!" from around the table, and something about James being a dork, the bell rang, indicating the end of the lunch period. I don't remember if the word "dork" was the exact descriptive used back then or not. But the meaning of whatever word we did use meant just about the same thing.

James Cortney Montgomery III never seemed to fit in with the rest of the kids, not just the kids in our class, but any other group of kids in the entire school. He always seemed to focus on what *he* had or what *he* did was always the best or at least a little better than anyone else. At times, but not very often, I somehow felt sorry for him because he always appeared to be very lonely. Nobody ever wanted to play or associate with him, at least not for very long. No sympathy from me on this particular day. Anyone who insulted my new bike, or those of my close friends, wouldn't receive any form of sympathy if I could help it.

A similar incident happened with the same James Cortney Montgomery III in high school. Many of my classmates worked for or were fortunate enough to have parents that provided us with our own vehicles, better known as "wheels" in high school. James managed to alienate us again because our VWs, used cars and trucks, and "junkyard specials" couldn't compare with his brand new fully-equipped Pontiac GTO. He called it his "muscle car." I wonder where James Cortney Montgomery III is today and what he's doing?

Status

Starting a new job and moving into a new town is quite an adventure, whether it's the first or tenth time. All the things that need to be done just to get settled into a new home can be overwhelming, like address changes, utility hookups, deciding where to grocery shop, meeting and making new friends, and just getting a feel for the community. Moving day is usually the official start of that process, at least at the new location. Oh sure, the house-hunting trip provided the anticipation of the move, but the physical move itself made the transfer *real*. When the moving van pulled up in front of the new house, I got the feeling our property suddenly became "center stage" and the community audience was anxiously waiting for the curtains to go up. The show was about to begin. The community is a relatively new suburban development with waterways and golf course intermixed. The curtains and blinds of neighboring houses appeared to be randomly opening and closing rather excessively throughout the day. The number of people walking their dogs, jogging, bicycle riding, and slowly driving by in their cars while not paying attention to the road, also seemed excessive. The movers who were manhandling our boxes and furniture were astute to notice. So for the fun of it, and without our being aware they were doing it, they decided to keep all our furniture covered and wrapped until safely in the house and out of sight of the rubber-neckers. Later, when I innocently asked them why they hadn't removed the protective pads from the furniture out near the truck, their response was, "We like to drive nosey neighbors crazy!" Jokingly they said they didn't want to embarrass us or themselves by letting our new neighbors see the "Early Salvation Army" and "Second Hand Store" furniture they were moving into our house. It worked! The part about driving some of the neighbors crazy.

Prior to the move, I didn't know a majority of the homes in the community were owned and occupied by various other management and "corporate" personnel from the company. Our home was originally a model home the developer built on

147

Personal Values

speculation. Naturally, everyone in the community knew the layout, square footage, types of appliances, number of phone jacks, and even the types of interior doors and windows we had. I was always amazed, and I'm sure it showed on my face, when colleagues would stop by my office and ask how we were going to decorate the family room, then provide a few of their own suggestions on how they would do it. I don't remember how many times we were asked if we liked using the Jacuzzi, or if the Jenn-Aire range top had adequate ventilation when using the built-in grill feature.

There should be a federal law, or at least a state law, stating during the first two months or so after a major cross-country move, guests are welcome at your home only if invited and/or pre-screened by the new homeowner. We'll agree the cakes and cookies are most welcome during the first few days, especially before the kitchen boxes are unpacked. Even though it *might* be a gesture of good will, the self-appointed neighborhood greeter expects you to invite her in as she's standing at your front door looking over your shoulder in anticipation and hopes of taking up the next three hours of your time. The timing of her gesture is generally unwelcome. I would bet that a potentially profitable cottage business would be the production of introductory videos for transferred or relocated families. A standardized template could be used where everyone, including the pets, could stand in front of the camera and individually tell their life history, model some of their favorite clothes, and together do a camera walkthrough of the new house, highlighting special features. Along the tour, every family member could tell favorite stories and memories about particular pieces of furniture or memorabilia. Such a tour would be similar to the First Lady's Annual Christmas Tour of the White House. Copies could be distributed to all the neighbors prior to or upon arrival in the new neighborhood, with a large brightly colored note requesting no cakes or cookies. In turn, if neighbors had extra copies from their last move, they could swap videos with the new arrivals, provided their move wasn't more than ten years prior.

In an effort to start meeting new friends and neighbors, along with developing social relationships with work colleagues, my wife and I decided to invite select business associates and neighbors over for an evening, either for dinner or maybe just cocktails and hors d'oeuvres. We would do this on those evenings when we were tired of unpacking boxes and trying to decide where to put everything. Why don't homes ever have enough storage space? During this process, parts of the house were still considered disaster zones and were definitely off limits for *any* guests. Notice I said "select" colleagues and neighbors! There were some individuals who didn't seem, at least at first, to fit into our "schedule," and probably never would.

After about three months of persistent and not necessarily subtle suggestions, one of the VPs at the office finally discarded his pseudo subtlety and bluntly asked if my wife and I would like to get together with him and his wife one evening. "How about some evening next week?" he responded. By now I realized he and his wife were neighbors and lived in the same development as we. He passed our home every day on his way to and from the office. I'm surprised he didn't suggest carpooling too. It's amazing how quickly we start to recognize and associate people with their cars, children, or pets. The typical, "Oh, so you're Billy's mother!" or "So you're the one in the green sport utility who waves and blows the horn every day." How nice, I thought, this would be our first invitation to someone's home since our arrival in town. We were getting the feeling the town in general was less than friendly. I said I would check with my wife to make sure her schedule permitted, but I suspected it would be fine. Even though he and his wife were nowhere near the top of *our* list of people we wanted to get to know immediately, he was still a "corporate" VP. In addition to being persistent over the past month or so, he appeared cordial enough and seemed to show a sincere interest in getting together, so why not.

After discussing the invitation with my wife and getting a little less than an enthusiastic "Well, okay" from her, the next morning I stopped by the VP's office and told him we would be pleased to get together. I explained that unfortunately the only day we had open was the following Tuesday evening. He said Tuesday would be great and, without pausing to take a breath, asked what time he and his wife should come over. That wasn't exactly the scenario I had anticipated. I now realized why my wife was hesitant in her response at first. Maybe there is such a thing as feminine intuition!

At exactly seven o'clock on Tuesday evening, Bob and Barbara Spencer rang the doorbell. I must admit, they were punctual. Upon opening the door, I immediately got the feeling my wife and I were underdressed for the occasion, even in our new home. Bob and Barbara were dressed as if they'd just returned from a front cover photo shoot for a fashion magazine. In comparison, my wife and I resembled the universal poster children for a charity organization seeking donations immediately following a natural disaster. As soon as we graciously welcomed them into our home and closed the front door, Bob asked, in what he thought was a joking manner, but to me was a condescending tone of voice, "It's safe to park my new *Beemer* in your driveway, isn't it?" Considering we lived less than two hundred yards away from each other, I assured him our "side of the tracks" was probably safe, at least for the evening. In jest, I offered to call the local police and request additional patrols for the remainder of the evening if he would feel more comfortable. For some unknown reason, Bob didn't see the humor in my response. First, what's a *Beemer,* and secondly, would you drive the equivalent of two hundred yards to visit with a neighbor?

The bottle of wine Bob proudly presented to my wife had a label printed in what appeared to be a fancy French script the United States Foreign Consulate to France probably couldn't read or understand. How fashionable, considering tonight would be the first time in years we needed to use a corkscrew. In fact, I wasn't sure if we had even unpacked the corkscrew. We're used to the twist off caps on gallon jugs or easy pour spouts on recycled cardboard boxes.

It was less than three minutes into the visit when my wife Wendy and I started glancing at each other and rolling our eyes. Over the years, married couples acquire the ability to communicate very well with each other using only their eyes or body posture, and we were perfecting that skill quite well, especially this evening. Wendy had one of those looks that asked, "Can we leave now?" The problem was, we were at our own home. Without saying a word to each other, we both knew and concurred it was probably going to be a long, long evening. I also knew from the way my wife starred at me and her particular forced smile, I was going to owe her, big time!

The dinner was delicious and wine superb. Serving the three courses provided a welcome distraction and opportunity to periodically remove ourselves from the one-way conversation. The direction of the entire evening's conversation was from the Spencers to the Matthews. The evening's discourse quickly developed a predictable pattern that dragged out over the next several hours. First, Bob or Barbara would ask a question. Second, my wife or I would attempt to respond with a complete short sentence. Third, Bob or Barbara would interrupt during the first few words of our response and proceed to talk about themselves. I started to think we were on the set for the filming of *"Lifestyles of the Rich and Famous"* with Bob and Barbara alternately sharing the role of commentator. Watch out Robin Leach, you might have competition soon!

By the time we served the main course, both Wendy and I came to the conclusion we've been leading very boring, mediocre, third-class lives in comparison to the Spencers and their social standards. There wasn't anything, and I do mean anything, we ever did, planned to do, owned, read, saw, visited, heard, or thought that Bob and Barbara couldn't top with their own fabulous story. At one point during dessert, however, the Spencer's continual striving for superiority status over the Matthews was almost shattered. Barbara noticed the diamond ring on my wife's finger, so rather than breaking the flow of the theme for the evening, we assured Barbara the stone was not really a diamond, but cubic zirconium. Barbara appeared quite relieved after hearing about the cubic zirconium. Wendy and I didn't want to ruin a *perfect* evening with the truth!

After dinner we moved to the family room to continue our lesson on third-class citizenship. Wendy and I quickly realized Bob and Barbara had to have been trained in surveillance techniques by the FBI. Their eyes scanned every nook and cranny of our entry, living room, kitchen, dining room, and family room. By our choice, those were the only rooms they were able to get access to. To our amazement, neither Bob nor Barbara used the bathroom that entire evening. In the course of the evening Barbara asked several times how we were progressing with the unpacking process "throughout the rest of the house." Considering all those boxes and other wrapped items that she noticed were unloaded from the van on moving day, she remarked unpacking must have been quite a formidable task. What she was really hinting at, each time she said anything about our move, was to be invited on a tour of the rest of our home. Without intending to, my eyes met my wife's eyes in a casual glance. Without having to utter a single word or convey the message via any other form of non-verbal communication, we both agreed a tour of the house for the Spencers was not on the agenda for this particular evening, or probably any other evening.

By the end of the evening's visit, my wife and I had verbal commitments from the Spencers that they would "just love" to sponsor us at the country club. By the end of the evening, that same invitation was extended to the yacht club, the athletic club, the tennis club, the rifle club, the sportsmen's club, and every other possible club and organization one could think of. We also received personal referrals to local restaurants where we were *granted permission* to use the Spencers' name to personally meet the chefs or owners.

On the way back to the front door, as they were preparing to leave, Barbara accidentally started walking down the hall toward another part of our home. Her error, to Wendy and me, seemed more calculated than accidental. We politely informed her of her *innocent* mistake. I guess our marbled entry, double doors and chandeliered vestibule could be mistaken for something other than an exit. The *Beemer* still appeared to have all its wheels and tires attached as we walked the Spencers to the driveway. Just before she closed the passenger door, Barbara said it was *our* turn to visit *them* at *their* home. Wendy and I simultaneously nodded in a gesture of our appreciation for the invitation. Without realizing at first we even did it, we simultaneously glanced at each other, in a loving and appreciative way, as our eyes rolled hopefully for the last time that evening. I could tell Wendy was thinking our cat would need brushed or the toilet bowls cleaned, just coincidentally, on that night, should such an invitation ever be extended. It's been several years and we have yet to receive the promised invitation.

We don't feel overly hurt or insulted by not having been invited to the Spencers' home. Wendy and I can't help but notice, considering the proximity of our homes, over the past several years since we moved into the community, the only regular visitor to the Spencers' home seems to be the periodic deliveries by the UPS or FedEx man. And for some reason, the

Spencers have alienated the neighbors on either side of their property, not to mention the rest of the community.

Whenever Wendy and I meet someone whose behavior even hints at being like the Spencers, we like to start asking them about their ancestors, bloodlines, and extended family members. Maybe there's a connection. To date we haven't found any relationship between the Spencers and James Cortney Montgomery III...

Chapter XII

Priorities

Good order is the foundation for all good things.
Burke 1729-1797

Who or what had the greatest positive influence on you in your life? And why?

If that question seems a little too vague or broad to answer, maybe I can position the question a little differently based on something I read in *Reader's Digest* a number of years ago. Let's assume it's your eightieth birthday and your family surprises you with a birthday party. As everyone is enjoying cake and ice cream, one of your grandchildren sits on your lap and poses the following question: "Grandpa, looking back over the things you've done or experienced in your lifetime, what would you say was the most important?" (Feel free to substitute "Grandma" for "Grandpa.") It's a tough question for those of us who consider ourselves in the prime of our years. It's interesting to note no matter what age you are, the definition of "prime" years and "older" keeps changing. Our answers would probably span from one end of the continuum to the other. Interestingly enough though, as you sample people in their sixties and seventies or beyond, their responses gradually become quite similar.

Growing up as a member of, and at the start of, what's now called the "baby boomer" generation, life was considerably different from what I see later generations (and the children of today) experiencing. Let's set one thing straight up front, our family was far removed from what was depicted on the *Ozzie and Harriet* or *Father Knows Best* television shows. I can't think of any family, at least in our community, that lived like that television fantasy. My father didn't wear a suit and tie while lounging around the house, nor did my mother dress as if expecting a personal visit at any moment from Martha Stewart. Ours was, however, what would be considered, in retrospect, a traditional family for that era. My father provided the sole support for the family while my mother took care of the children and most household matters. Their conservative views in political and financial matters seem to have taken root. Even to this day, I purchase nothing on credit. The philosophy we grew up with was first to save for what you want, then go buy it, not the other way around. Additionally, education was a priority for my sisters and me, along with assuming and developing the responsibility for taking care of oneself. None of us had the choice about *if* we were going to go on to college. The only choice we had any say-so in was where we would go to get our undergraduate degrees.

My oldest sister was very involved in girl scouting throughout her youth, which meant my mother became a Girl Scout leader, whether she wanted to or not. She was a woman who appreciated modern conveniences, so bugs and sleeping in tents wasn't quite her definition of a good time. But organizing the annual cookie sales, serving as a chaperone for events, and fulfilling the role of chauffeur usually qualified her on an annual basis for an embroidered badge and framed certificate of appreciation from the troop. Both the badges and certificates were hand crafted by the girls in the troop. For reasons unknown to me at the time, she never wore the badges in public other than to Girl Scout activities like the annual Memorial Day parade or during fundraisers. Girl Scout cookie season was always a great time of the year. The family cars were removed from the garage and relegated to the driveway for a month or two because the garage was stacked to the ceiling with pallets of cookies. I was never permitted to raid any of the boxes, but somehow just knowing such a treasure of tasty treats was sitting on the other side of the garage door was enough to make any kid respond like Pavlov's dogs. Dad wasn't much into participating at the girls' meetings, fundraisers, or other stuff like that, but he did handle the masculine chores, like stacking cookie boxes and repairing camping equipment. He never received a badge or certificate of appreciation from the troop, but it didn't seem to matter to him.

Like my mother, my next oldest sister didn't find girl scouting very attractive or appealing. Her sentiments and comments about girl scouting usually focused on the fact she "...didn't like to do dirt." Even to this day, she still lives life by that same philosophy. For a while, her destiny seemed focused and headed towards the New York Theater District and the fine arts. With the stated ambition to become a *prima ballerina* with the Russian Ballet, or whatever ballet troupe was in vogue at the time, Saturday mornings were reserved for tap dance and ballet lessons. Her dedication, even as a child, seemed to be genuine. Every waking moment of every day, for months on end, she could be found walking and jumping *à pointe* all around the house. As the younger brother who was considered too young and immature to trust at home by himself on Saturday mornings, I found myself also enrolled in the same ballet and tap dance lessons. The tap and ballet lessons really were fun and a great opportunity to socialize with a lot of different kids our age, but there was a down side. The most humiliating part of the weekly Saturday morning *cultural* experience was having to wear brightly colored tights and matching top. Keep in mind this was in the early fifties when "men" didn't wear pink tights. At that time, I envisioned myself more as a jeans and cowboy boots type of guy. John Wayne was more of role model for me than Mikhail Baryshnikov ever could have been. The humiliation was probably worth bearing, considering the pride in our parents' eyes during our first recital.

Just like my sisters, I had many diverse interests and participated in various activities as a kid, all of which held higher priorities than ballet and tap lessons, at least in my mind. Any outdoor activities and sports seemed to occupy a majority of my time. For a while, little league baseball became a passion, even though I never got a single hit during my first year on the team. We could have given the "Bad News Bears" a run for their money, not for our playing abilities, but because we gave new meaning to the word *bad.* I remember our desperate coach philosophizing and telling the entire team we could be the league's champions if we put our minds to it and if we dedicated ourselves to individual and team practice. I took his words seriously and would practice running bases and sliding into home plate for hours on end. I must have worn out three bats one summer just hitting stones into the lake. Stones didn't need to be chased like a baseball did, especially if you hit them into the water. My philosophy was to dedicate more time and energy to hitting, no matter what it was, than to spending time chasing a ball. Even though we had a losing season that year, we still managed to achieve a place in the record books with our perfect "no win" season. One redeeming event after such a record season was the league picnic and having our pictures taken in our full dress uniforms. We proudly stuck out our chests so everyone could read the name of our team, the

"Yankees." In spite of my season's no hit record, my parents made every game and cheered us on.

Even though my sisters and I had our individual interests and activities while growing up, except maybe for the forced ballet and tap lessons, there was also a common thread at home that seemed to provide some of the foundation for all of our future successes and individual achievements. Just like the times when we get together today and reminisce, that common thread always surfaces. Even though we didn't realize it during our formative years, the interest and involvement our parents showed in our activities provided that foundation. They were responsible, whether intentionally or not, for the many wonderful memories and mysterious bonds that makes a family so meaningful. Their involvement or participation in all the "special" events in our lives was critical, but even more important were the day to day little things they did. Their efforts may seem to have gone unnoticed by us kids at the moment, but their effects have lasted a lifetime.

All throughout grade school, even though we were sometimes a little rushed in the mornings, breakfast together was a must. No excuses! Notice I said "together." It was a time to share what our day was going to be like. Even though time around the breakfast table was cut short on many mornings because of varying schedules, we knew any unfinished conversations would be able to be continued later in the day. Dinner could be considered a daily ritual, but again in a positive sense. No, we didn't pattern our lives after or look anything like *The Walton's* family dinner scenes as depicted on television. Our evening dinners were a mandatory daily family activity with little tolerance for being absent. As we got older and became more involved in our various school and outside activities, planning dinner was a little more difficult, but every attempt was made to accommodate everyone's busy schedules. Dinner was a family affair where everyone did a mini-debrief of his day's events.

Back in the early fifties, families with a television set in the home were in the minority. Notice I said "a" television set, not three or four randomly scattered throughout the house like most homes have today. At the time, we were fortunate to be part of that minority. In fact, the living room was specifically arranged so the television set was the focal point for every seat in the room. Unfortunately the same is true today in most homes, but for a different reason. Our television was not used as a substitute baby sitter or sole form of entertainment. When we watched television, it was a family affair. When the television was turned on, usually the program selection was made by consensus and the entire family participated in a democratic decision-making process. By default, the selection process was rather simple back then because there were only three networks and one educational channel available. As far as family entertainment was concerned, the most risqué scene a child was exposed to was Ozzie and Harriet turning off the light as they went to sleep in separate beds, still fully clothed. I can recall many evenings when the television was never turned on in our house. What happened after we fell asleep, I'm not sure. On those "television off" nights, Mom and Dad would divert our attention by reading stories to us from some of our favorite books. We would snuggle closely together on the floor right in front of the fireplace, intently listening and eventually falling asleep in weird positions only kids can manage to get into. Mysteriously, we would wake up the next morning in our own beds. Many cold winter nights were spent in front of the fireplace (our house did have central heating, I'm not that old) playing board games where we all, as a family, were involved. Seems I usually lost while my sisters usually won all the various games we played. I would attribute losing to my age and being inexperienced. Funny thing was, somehow Mom and Dad always seemed to lose too. They always seemed to make absent-minded mistakes, usually near the end of the game, preventing them from ever being victorious. I always figured I was in good company. Once my sisters and I, prior to one evening's fireside game playing, decided to intentionally let our parents win, sort of like "customer golf." Would you believe they still managed to lose!

Without any of us kids realizing it at the time, our parents made a special effort to always attend or participate in most, if not all, of our school and outside activities. Whether it was watching us during ballet and tap lessons (Yuck!) or honoring us with flowers at the opening night recital, they were always there to support and encourage us to do our best. Short of totally rescheduling their activities, nothing would get in the way of major events like our birthday parties, sporting events, plays, picnics, and anything else important to us kids. Even as we grew older, our parents' participation in our lives was usually most appreciated. Oh sure, we also went through stages where we didn't want to be seen with our parents for various reasons, just like all other kids, but those times were few and far between. Later we realized, the benefit from their participation was a two-way street. As we were growing up, they provided the foundation for memories that will last our lifetime, and in turn, they received the rewards and satisfaction of being a part of their children's development and successes, along with a few disappointments.

Dennis Lawrence could probably be classified as a traditional "company man." Having climbed the ladder of success within the same company for his entire career, he was eventually promoted to Vice President about six years ago. In his mid to late fifties, he is a very intense and driven man. When I came on board with the company, he seemed to take a personal interest in me, and in turn, I enjoyed working and interacting with him. He had an historical perspective of the company, which I found invaluable during my first few months' learning curve, as I was finding out about this company's idiosyncrasies and "corporate" politics. Over my first year or two, Dennis and I developed a wonderful working relationship where we could bounce ideas, various thoughts, and other topics of concern off each other. We developed a strong and genuine personal trust in each other and seemed to intuitively know where the other was coming from. What was unique about our relationship was how we could provide direct and "honest" feedback on any number of sensitive business or personal issues. I'm not talking about sharing our darkest and deepest secrets, but being able to serve as personal mentors and coaches for each other.

Dennis seemed to have the drive and enthusiasm to never back off or quit once he got headed in a particular direction. He dedicated, what seemed to me, an inordinate amount of time to fulfilling his duties and responsibilities at the office. He would schedule business trips that regularly extended into the weekends, or, in some cases, into holidays. Very rarely did he ever schedule and take vacation days off. His work seemed to energize him. The more he traveled and worked, the more driven he became. He would be the kind of subordinate any manager would fantasize about having work for him. The company more than got its money's worth out of him.

To the casual observer, Dennis' work and dedication sure was paying off. He was part of the executive team and reported directly to the President. He was providing for his family the material things some people only dream about and strive their whole lives to achieve. He owned a beautiful home in an exclusive part of town, three new automobiles, retirement investments, a country club membership, and just about every modern convenience, novelty, and appliance you could think of. I suspect he owned every $19.95 plastic kitchen utensil or household trinket ever advertised on television. Veg-a-Matic and Ginsu knives included!

After I worked with Dennis for about a year, there came a period of time when he seemed a little more tense and stressed than usual. One day I specifically made the effort to ask him about the sudden change in his demeanor I thought I noticed. He listened intently to what I had to say then attributed his behavior to his added workload and the annual peak-season problems his department was experiencing. One morning as I arrived at the office, Dennis met me in the hall near my office door. He had a look on his face anyone could read and interpret very accurately. Something serious was on his mind and he needed to talk about it now, not later. I left my briefcase on my desk and walked directly to his office. As I sat down, Dennis closed the door and then sat behind his desk. This had to be very serious, because we rarely closed our doors, especially at this time of the morning before anyone else was in the building. Knowing he'd been on a business trip for the last five days or so, I was starting to wonder if one of his major business deals had gone sour. He wasn't even attempting to joke around like we usually did most mornings.

What he said next caught me completely by surprise, and what a shock! With a tired and drained look on his face, he said when he'd returned home from his business trip last night, he arrived to find an empty house. And when he said empty, he meant just that, empty! All the furniture was moved out of the house. His wife and children were nowhere to be found. And as he walked through the house in a stupor, he found a scribbled note from his wife stating divorce papers were in the process of being drawn up and would be served on him shortly. There wasn't much I could think to say at this point, but what I figured I could do was listen and serve as a sounding board. This wasn't a time to take sides or make any kind of value judgments. There are always two sides to every story, and who knows, things still could possibly get straightened out between him and his wife. Fortunately for me, I didn't have to say much. Dennis did most of the talking for the next few hours.

Seems Dennis and his wife had been having problems for quite some time. It was something I suspected, but he never brought up the subject, so I never inquired, except for the one time I asked him about the change in his demeanor. In looking back, obvious warning signs were more than apparent, but for some reason neither I, nor anyone else, recognized them for what they were. Whether his dedication to his work contributed to the family problems or the family problems contributed to his excessive concentration on his job, is something only he can answer. Somehow to me, it seemed like a vicious spiral where one probably escalated the other.

For me, the rest of the day carried a heavy dark cloud over it; I'm sure not as dark as the cloud Dennis was experiencing. Not only could I feel the pain Dennis was going through, but I also couldn't stop wondering if or how his dedication to his work and business life might have contributed to the problems. Even though the "gospel spoken from the executive offices" professes the need to balance one's personal and work life, little accommodation is ever made, or consideration given, to the quality of personal life at all levels throughout the corporation. The culture rewards "dedication" to the company, and according to Dennis it always has, with little if any regard for an employee's personal and family life. An annual company picnic and a frozen turkey at Thanksgiving or Christmas doesn't qualify as contributing to the quality of or balance in an employee's work and personal life.

The following year was very difficult on Dennis. After several unsuccessful attempts at reconciliation, the divorce proceedings drug out for months. Living in a "community property" state, according to Dennis, meant most of the property and assets accumulated in many years of marriage, were going to end up at the "other" community. During this period of lawyer meetings and legal maneuvering, Dennis started to dedicate even more time to business travel and long hours working at the office. We continued to talk on a semi-regular basis as the divorce proceedings moved at a snail's pace. It was obvious the process of getting his life back on track was proving to be a challenge, and in all probability, a long one at that. One thing became perfectly clear to me. Dennis could deal with the division and loss of most of the material possessions and wealth he and his wife accumulated over the years. But sadly, on the other hand, the loss and continued deterioration of his relationship with his children had no price. During the time the divorce was being finalized, Dennis would periodically reflect on how many of his children's birthdays he missed over the years because of a business trip! He could easily count on one hand the number of evenings a year he dedicated exclusively to quality time with his family and children. He never once attended any extra-curricular activities his children were involved with. He sadly came to realize he didn't really know his children, and in turn, they didn't know him.

The old saying that "misery loves company" provides little consolation in Dennis' case. During the same period Dennis was going through his divorce, four others within the corporate office were in the same situation, each showing similar characteristics of being or becoming workaholics. Maybe it's a sign of the times, but upon further review of the corporate directory, there were more "corporate" managers who went through at least one divorce while employed by this company than those with happy first marriages.

Over the past three plus years, Dennis has been slowly getting his life back in order. He's still spending as much time as ever, if not more, working and traveling for business. I'm sure it's a diversion for his energies at this point in his life. Working probably helps to keep his mind occupied, preventing him from becoming completely depressed. His strained relations with his children remain just that, strained. Unfortunately, the opportunities and time needed to reestablish a strong bond with his grown children are limited at best, and sadly, he knows it.

For Dennis, regular retirement at age sixty-five is less than a decade away, and even sooner should he be *able* to financially swing an early retirement, which is unlikely since the divorce. Given the financial losses as a result of the divorce, and a few questionable decisions he made after the divorce was final, early retirement might not be possible. One of the topics we now seem to talk about rather frequently centers around what each of us wants to do after retirement. Both of us have a need to be productive in our own way, realizing an extended diet of golf or fishing wouldn't be fulfilling. For Dennis, retirement wasn't a topic he gave serious consideration to until recently. He can now tell you without hesitation how many more days, not years, before he can retire. But between now and then, his stated goal is to concentrate on developing a better balance between his work and personal life. I'm not real confident he'll be successful. It's difficult to change fifty year old habits and modify a lifestyle he's been accustomed to.

The company has grown quickly over the past several years, producing an ever-expanding corporate structure and an inefficient bureaucracy. Because of a number of acquisitions, the pool of VPs has disproportionately expanded. Organizationally the company is adding "corporate" and executive layers. There was a time when Dennis reported directly to the President; today he's two levels removed from the President and rarely even sees him anymore. What a classic case study for the *Harvard Business School!* Dennis now sees everything he's worked for over the years gradually slipping away, and the *company* couldn't care less...

Today, if someone asked Dennis the question, "...in looking back over the things you've done or experienced in your lifetime, what would you say was the most important?" I wonder how he would answer.

Chapter XIII

Procrastination

Procrastination is the thief of time.
Young 1683-1765

I called my oldest sister this past week to find out if she and her husband had anything planned for the upcoming Thanksgiving weekend. Spending holidays together and bonding with family members is gradually becoming more and more enjoyable and nostalgic. Not that family members weren't enjoyable to be with before, but as we mature, and I use that word loosely, holidays seem to be taking on an entirely different meaning. With the four-day weekend and two sides of the family to accommodate, my wife's and mine, making arrangements to get together with parents and immediate family can, at times, be a logistical nightmare. Sometimes I'm convinced the organizers of the annual Rose Bowl Parade experience less coordination and logistical problems while working with hundreds of thousands of people than we do accommodating a dozen family members around the dining room table. Now don't get me wrong, I'm not complaining, placing blame, or pointing fingers at anyone. It's just that everyone seems to have his own agenda with his own idiosyncratic approach to holiday planning and getting together. It reminds me of the underlying theme behind the training video entitled *The Abilene Paradox*. The bottom line in the video demonstrates how we usually get caught up in a process called *mismanaged agreement*. We all agree we want to get together, but because of our inability to manage the agreement process, we end up doing, in some circumstances, just the opposite of what we all wanted to do in the first place. We do eventually get together sometime over the holiday weekend, but only after the running around, feasting on identical dinners at several homes over four days, and a thousand more miles racked up on the car's odometer. By the end of the four days, we're all usually giving thanks the Thanksgiving weekend is over. And just think, the Christmas and New Year's holidays are only a month later!

I might make it sound like holidays are a time of unnecessary tension and stress within our family, but they really aren't. They have always been a time of fun and joy, and have provided the memories future holiday conversations are based on. Over the years we've come to recognize the process for what it really is, but it still continues. The process, that is. Collectively or individually, and even when we know better, it seems old patterns, personal agendas, and lifelong habits are sometimes difficult to change.

After the typical "Hi, how are you?" and "Did I catch you at a bad time?" questions when my sister answered the phone, I asked her what she and her husband were doing with their long and dark November evening. Have you noticed that for about the first week or two after resetting our clocks from Daylight Savings Time to Standard Time, we experience a kind of non-alcoholic hangover? It's a period of a few days to a week when we experience a complete readjustment in our body's biorhythms, both physically and mentally. And for some of us, it's probably more mental than physical.

Her response to my question was interesting, even though she never really answered it directly. She said she had a report due for work the next day and needed to complete it that evening. But instead of taking the hour or so necessary to complete the report, she said she was successfully finding and accomplishing many other unrelated and unnecessary domestic and household tasks. For reasons only known to her, they demanded her attention and seemed to take priority over doing the report. Naturally, I did the inappropriate thing and asked what those other distractions were, even though I honestly didn't care. It was one of those questions we ask for no better reason than to ask it. Even though she knew her response was going to show how irrational her behavior was, she continued to tell me anyway. With a smile in her voice, she gave me a list of about twenty things she chose to occupy her time that evening. Her list included brushing the cat, cleaning toilets, rearranging the underwear drawer, refilling the salt and pepper shakers, alphabetizing the canned goods in the pantry, updating the address book, and many other "high priority" activities. What's so intriguing about her response is she knew what *needed* to be done, but wasn't doing it. It's generally not her style to put things off. She knew the potential negative consequences of her report not being completed on time, but as she said, she "couldn't help it." What she was actually saying was, she didn't care to do the report in the first place. Even our phone conversation that evening had the feel of longevity and the potential of never ending. During most of our other phone conversations, we don't talk for extended periods of time, but tonight was one of those conversations that had the potential to drag on and on and on. Not because I had a need to talk, but because she was looking for another reason to justify not working on the report. Whatever motivating reasons she had, the activities she was engaging in that evening seemed more attractive and compelling than completing that darn report. Such behavior is not limited to just my sister. I'll lay odds you and almost everyone you know, suffer at times from the same affliction.

When I was a fourth grader in Miss Kassil's class at Lyndora School, one of my first very memorable lessons with procrastination occurred. The sequence of events and what subsequently happened contributed to the many vivid and permanent memories etched into my brain. Oh sure, like any kid, I could put off doing things I didn't want to do, but this fourth grade experience was one of those significant emotional events family folklore is eventually made of. And I do mean "family," because by the time all was said and done, my whole family, to some extent, was involved. We regularly bring the incident up and fortunately, I can laugh about it today. As the years go by, we enhance the facts more and more, and are starting to believe the newly embellished and ever-modified story. However, at the time it happened I didn't find any humor in it at all.

It was the week of Thanksgiving, and to a fourth grader that meant we had only three days of school, Monday, Tuesday, and Wednesday. Then we could enjoy a four-day vacation with a holiday thrown in as a bonus, not to mention the anticipation of eating all the turkey, cranberry sauce, and pumpkin pie. To a nine-year old, what more could one ask for out of life? Looking in retrospect, I'm sure the three-day school week proved most challenging for our teachers. You too can no doubt recall the amount of learning taking place during Thanksgiving week was probably minimal. Usually by the end of November in Western Pennsylvania, the first significant snowfall has already taken place, and cold weather seriously limits the number of days students can be outdoors on the playground during recess. But this particular year was a meteorological exception. The Wednesday before Thanksgiving proved to be a bright sunny day with no wind, and a temperature reading in the low sixties. Recess outside usually consisted of the girls huddling together next to the school building, talking and giggling. The boys usually organized some "manly" game or semi-sporting activity. On this Wednesday before Thanksgiving, about ten of us decided to play tag. One person would be "it," which no one wanted to be, and his role in the game was to chase the other players and gently touch one of them. When the person who was "it" touched the individual that he caught, he would holler out loud, "you're it!" The touched person, and I mean that in a positive way, would then, as the name of the game indicated, be "it." The person who was "it" was then expected to chase any of the others who were playing and try to tag one of them. This simple game could go on for hours. The object of the game was to keep from being tagged, thus avoiding being "it." And if you were "it," the intent was to catch and tag someone else as quickly as possible. As sophisticated fourth graders, we usually played within agreed upon geographical boundaries, which consisted of imaginary lines from the corner of the school building to a specified wild cherry tree, to a wooden post near the teacher's parking lot, and back to another corner of the building.

Today my recollection of the *exact* events that happened that day are a little vague, and I'm sure somewhat intentionally repressed. A good friend at the time, Paul Price, was "it." He started randomly chasing the rest of us, but couldn't seem to make the tag. Sure, we teased him, because that was all part of the game, wasn't it? Paul was a little slower in his running than the rest of us. One strategy we frequently utilized, to keep from being "it" for too long, was to seek out Paul and tag him. Why not? He was obviously a slow easy target and was always willing to play. My version of the story and subsequent events that happened that bright fall day goes something like this:

I was within bounds, but near the corner of our imaginary playing field and Paul was coming on fast, fast in this case considering the limited amount of in-bounds real estate remaining to us. No problem. I could outmaneuver him with a body fake and a quick buttonhook move in the other direction. As I gracefully attempted to dodge him, I slipped, started to fall, and unexpectedly got smacked across the side of my head with Paul's closed fist. I'm sure, and Paul reassures me to this day, the forceful contact wasn't intentional, but circumstantial. My instinctive reaction to the painful knock on the side of the head was an overreaction. For a moment, the pain of being clobbered caused big tears to well up in my eyes. Now keep in mind, fourth grade boys are too macho to cry, especially around one's friends, and even more importantly, in front of the on-looking girls. To add insult to injury, I was more annoyed I'd been tagged by Paul, especially since he was the slowest runner in class, even slower than most of the girls. Now that's embarrassing! Secondly, I couldn't be seen crying, because the humiliation would be much worse and more enduring than the actual physical pain I was experiencing. So I did what any fourth grade boy would do! I quickly got up pretending nothing was wrong. Because Paul was still close by and sincerely apologizing for having hit me by accident, I decided to tag him back before he got too far away. With both my arms swinging and the tightly closed fist of my right hand, I returned the favor by "tagging" Paul on the side of his head. Mohammed Ali would have been impressed! After a short tussle during which Paul and I hit each other a few more times and hollered a number of "Oh, Yeahs!" accompanied by a little mild profanity, the game continued, but not for long.

Upon observing our primitive and uncultured exhibition of masculine behavior, and unknown to Paul and me at the time, one of the girls ran inside the school and reported to our teacher a major brawl was unfolding outside. Miss Kassil was a big woman, at least from our point of view, and legend had it she was once a professional wrestler. Well before the recess bell rang, both Paul and I were conveniently escorted by our collars back into the building. The firm grip on our collars was a message in itself, but not having our feet touch the ground for the whole trip back into the school building was an unquestionable indication of "big" trouble. I do remember the looks of awe and amazement from all the other kids still on the playground as we were literally "air lifted" indoors, directly back to our classroom. For weeks afterwards, rumors and stories continued about Miss Kassil and how she manhandled both Paul and me.

Back then, teachers handled their own disciplinary problems. A trip to the principal's office was more of a negative reflection on the teacher than on the misbehaving student. In addition, both Paul's and my parents would have supported any punishment Miss Kassil might have meted out, then the same or worse would probably happen again when we got home. After tearfully providing our individual versions of the alleged fight, which, by the way, were almost identical, Paul and I each had a choice to make. We could receive several swats with "The Paddle" or write five hundred times the phrase "Fighting in school is not allowed!" Considering Miss Kassil's fearsome reputation and the size of "The Paddle" sitting on the corner file cabinet, we both decided to become better versed in our writing skills. Why not? We had until Monday morning, after the four-day holiday break, to turn in our punishment.

Even with my limited experience with project planning skills back then, writing six words five hundred times should have been relatively easy. Five hundred divided by the five available evenings between Wednesday and Monday morning came out to only one hundred sentences a night, or the equivalent of writing six hundred words. The only logistical problem was deciding how to do the writing without my sisters and parents finding out why I was writing the sentence "Fighting in school is not allowed." Like any nine-year old, I was determined and convinced I could keep the incident a secret, at least from my family. What a mistake!

Personal Values

Wednesday evening didn't work out very well considering the volume of holiday company and relatives that stopped by our house that night. And with all the excitement of planning and preparing for the next day's Thanksgiving dinner, there wasn't time to think about being literary. No problem! Five hundred divided by four still came out to only one hundred twenty-five sentences to be written each evening, or seven hundred fifty words a day.

Thanksgiving night found the house filled with guests and numerous relatives unexpectedly stopping by to visit, as they did every year. Unfortunately, for some reason I wasn't personally informed such was the plan, nor did I remember or factor in Thanksgivings past. Okay, but now maybe I needed to start considering another approach to getting my writing done. Let's see, five hundred divided by three comes out to approximately one hundred sixty-seven sentences an evening, or one thousand two words. In theory that was very doable, but I realized the next day, to my misfortune, it was another tactical mistake! Friday was my birthday and the traditional surprise party my parents arranged for me lasted longer than I had anticipated. Now what fourth grader do you know would suggest breaking up his birthday party early to complete a school assignment?

When I woke up early on Saturday morning, the first thing on my mind was the mathematical reality that five hundred divided by two comes out to two hundred fifty, or one thousand five hundred words. Unless my calculations were wrong, time would be of the essence. I even calculated I needed to write three thousand words in the next forty-eight hours, which if my math was right, came out to sixty-two and a half words per hour. When you break that down into minimalist terms, that came out to slightly over one word a minute. Still, that didn't sound too bad, yet!

Finally, Saturday night and no company or family plans, just a quiet evening at home in front of the fireplace. We usually read or played games as a family, so I figured my cover story would be a good one. I would keep my writing covered the entire time, and if asked, I would respond by saying I was writing some poetry. My reasoning was based on the assumption that because poetry should be considered personal in nature, I preferred to keep it confidential until I was ready to publish it. Mixing poetry and me was like mixing water and oil, and everyone in my family knew it, except me.

After getting *the* six-word sentence written approximately twenty-six times, the inquiries and abuse I was enduring from the rest of the family was unbearable. Did I mention covering a sheet of paper where every line was identical was becoming difficult for this fourth grader, and very suspicious for the rest of the family? Try it, you'll see. Suddenly it occurred to me. Yes, that's it! I would get up in the middle of the night, while everyone else was sleeping, and whip this project out in no time. Have you *ever* heard of a nine-year-old, or any other kid unless he's sick, getting up in the middle of the night without an alarm? It doesn't happen!

Sunday morning and there were still four hundred seventy-four more sentences to write, or two thousand eight hundred forty-four words. By mid-afternoon, I started to realize the pressure was really on, so I retreated to my bedroom and began by writing number twenty-seven. When my mother called everyone for dinner, I was up to number one hundred seventeen. Things weren't progressing as well as I'd anticipated, and my writing was getting less and less legible. Right after dinner, I completely closed my bedroom door and resumed my literary career. Another major mistake! Very rarely did any of us ever close our bedroom doors. I was on number one hundred forty-one when my sister came barreling through the door into my room, asking what I was doing. The

Personal Values

poetry story didn't work this time, because with sleight of hand, she managed to grab one of the pages and dash out of the room. Sisters aren't always as kind and supportive to their younger brothers as maybe they should be. Needless to say, she shared my "literary masterpiece" with my parents.

No, I didn't even make it to one hundred fifty that night, nor did I turn in what portion I'd already completed the next morning. My parents took control of the situation. Sunday night was a very restless night for me. I spent Monday's lunch period *in conference* with Miss Kassil, and my parents. Suffice it to say, all five hundred sentences, or three thousand words, were turned in early on Tuesday morning!

Wade Harmon was the kind of person everybody liked, and I do mean everybody. In all the years I've been with the company, I've never heard anyone say he didn't like Wade. He was just a "nice guy." Even if you had a disagreement with him or if both of you were at polar opposites on an issue, Wade had this way about himself that still made you like him. He was a very dedicated "corporate" manager, and had been with the company for almost fifteen years. Even though most people suspected he was very unhappy in his present job, he never "openly" showed or talked about his dissatisfaction. It didn't help matters much that his wife and family disliked living in the town. They regularly encouraged Wade to request a transfer to another out-of-state facility or to make a job change. But a change for Wade will probably never be in the cards with this company, at least until he retires. For the immediate future his promotional opportunities within his department, and the company for that matter, were very limited. The way the company's retirement and stock programs work, after about ten years, an employee can't afford to leave without incurring major financial losses. Intentional or not, that's an interesting way for a company to retain employees. Not necessarily smart, but interesting! Unfortunately, such a system retains not only the good employees, but the less desirable ones too, and there were enough of them being retained and filling valuable office space.

A number of us in the "corporate" office were identified and subsequently invited by one of the board members to participate in a targeted sales initiative, a project that would focus on the company's top strategic accounts. The targeted accounts represented over fifty percent of the corporation's total annual sales. The project was supposed to be a joint effort primarily driven by marketing and sales, with secondary input from customer service, and the quality departments. Wade was delegated the responsibility of representing the customer service department. The VP for Customer Service, whom Wade reported to, had a reputation for delegating assignments to his subordinates, especially when he felt those assignments didn't provide "high exposure" or carry the type of "status" the VP felt he was worthy of. In this case, and to give the VP the benefit of the doubt, he also knew he didn't have the practical working knowledge for such a project. Even though he was the VP for Customer Service, he knew very little of what went on within his division. In his defense, he wasn't very different from many of the other VPs in the company. Probably most influential in his decision to send Wade was he knew, to put it mildly, his own personal working relationship with sales management was very stressed. Because the customer service department had a comprehensive customer database and Wade was familiar with its' operation, Wade's representation would be critical to the success of the initiative. Wade would be the one who retrieved most of the necessary data from the database. He was a good choice considering he also was well-liked by everyone on the sales force and all the others on the project team.

Personal Values

During the planning and early stages of the implementation meetings, there seemed to be an excessive amount of time dedicated to delineating individual responsibilities and determining completion dates for every assignment. Well, why not? This was a very critical project that could have long-lasting impacts and implications for future sales growth. Throughout the meetings, Dave, who chaired the initiative, was very deliberate, almost to the point of overkill, about making sure everyone understood exactly what was expected of him. Dave would go out of his way to accommodate any potential problem areas that surfaced or were raised by anyone in the group. For this particular project to be successful, everyone had to effectively pull his own load, and to make matters worse, within very tight time constraints. Any weak links in the planned chain of events for this initiative could spell failure and the potential loss of substantial financial resources dedicated to the project, and loss of future sales.

As part of my role in the initiative, I needed a number of items from Wade and his department before I could get started. With Dave's focus on up-front planning and his insistence on developing a comprehensive and detailed timeline for the total project, I left all the meetings confident everyone knew exactly what needed to be done.

Being a little compulsive about my responsibilities, not only in this project, but just about everything I do, I mentioned to Wade that my department would appreciate receiving any materials he was responsible for prior to the agreed upon deadline date, if possible. I told him that even if his materials were not in final format, we could at least look them over and possibly avert any unexpected future problems, thus assuring we would all be able to keep on schedule. Wade was most agreeable and promised at least a portion of the materials would be forwarded to me well ahead of schedule. Gosh, he sure was accommodating and a pleasure to work with! People were right; he sure is a nice guy and a team player!

It was a week before Wade was supposed to provide me the materials my team needed to get rolling. We were literally at a standstill until we got them. Even though there was still a week left before the agreed upon date for Wade to make delivery, I thought I would again ask him if he could provide "any" of the materials ahead of schedule. I even offered the services of my people to help expedite his processes, if necessary. Wade was very appreciative of my offer, but said everything was still on target. Well, I guess I was a little anxious to get started, and didn't need to be pressuring him the way I was. He seemed to understand my position and assured me I wasn't being a pest.

On the day Wade was supposed to provide my department with the materials he committed to, he was nowhere to be found. Finally, late in the afternoon, after numerous attempts, I did catch up with him in his office with the door closed. He was overly apologetic as he informed me the materials were "not quite ready yet." He figured he could have them completed by the following week. Putting aside diplomacy and tact, I specifically asked why he and his people hadn't made the deadline. In no uncertain terms, I let him know he'd just placed me and my team behind the eight ball. Wade fumbled for words and probably wore out a pair of shoes dancing around the question. In my opinion, the reasons he gave and the other priority projects he said he and his department were working on, instead of the customer initiative, could be classified in the same category as those my sister used for not doing her report.

After eventually gaining my composure again, I pinned Wade down on the date and time he would complete his part of the project, then proceeded immediately to Dave's office. Even though I was angry and disappointed the materials weren't ready, somehow Wade had this ability to pacify me. For whatever reason, I wasn't angry with him, just disappointed. He's just a nice guy.

Dave calmly permitted me to rant and rave for about two minutes, until I blew off all my steam. Dave wasn't surprised in the least about the situation, nor did he show any major annoyance with Wade. In a very controlled voice, Dave said he knew and expected such a thing would happen on this project with Wade "because that's just the way Wade is." Dave said everyone just *loves* Wade, but added everyone who's worked with him in the past also knows he *never* completes or follows-up with what he says or agrees to. Dave went on to say nothing he's ever tried in the past, from threats to talking with his manager, seems to work with Wade. "Sometimes," Dave said, "if Wade agrees to do something in the presence of other managers, it *might* get done." That's why during the planning process for this project Dave went to such great lengths to get group consensus and buy-in. His efforts were specifically directed towards Wade. And I thought those were Dave's normal project management skills coming out. In this case, it didn't work.

The next morning Dave called a meeting with Wade, Wade's VP, and me. Wade agreed to complete his part of the project by the very next morning.

When I arrived in the office the day after the "Dave, Wade, and Wade's VP" summit, all the promised materials were on my desk. I wonder if it would help if Wade had to write five hundred times "Not completing projects on time is unacceptable."

Chapter XIV

The More You Know...

Where is the Life we have lost in living?
Where is the wisdom we have lost in knowledge?
Where is the knowledge we have lost in information?
Elliot 1888-1965

The more you know, the more you know you don't know! I'm sure you've heard this line before, or at least something similar to it. Or possibly you may have heard something like the following: *Children keep trying the impossible, because they don't know yet that it can't be done!* For me, these two sayings compliment each other. At some point in life, we have all come to the conclusion that even though we might consider ourselves fairly well trained or educated, reality finally strikes. We eventually realize one person cannot possibly master even a small fraction of the vast amount of knowledge that exists out there. Some people recognize that fact early on, while others... Well, what can I say? New discoveries continue, at an exponential rate, to expand the boundaries of knowledge available to us. And just like children, we keep trying the *impossible,* pushing the boundaries and exploring the edges of discovery to find that *it can be done!*

Looking to the future with blinders on isn't something that's happened only in the distant past. Looking at both the past and present, influential political and business leaders have and will continue to view the world with their personal blinders on. I agree it's very difficult to predict the future, however I find it even more interesting that many very progressive and prominent business leaders have been bound by their own paradigms. Here are just a few I ran across in various magazines, books, and even on the World Wide Web:

> "This 'telephone' has too many shortcomings to be seriously considered as a means of communications. The device is inherently of no value to us."
> *-WESTERN UNION*
> *Internal Memo, 1876*

> "Everything that can be invented has been invented."
> *-CHARLES H. DUELL*
> *Commissioner*
> *U.S. Office of Patents, 1899*

> "Airplanes are interesting toys but of no military value."
> *-MARSHALL FERDINAND FOCH*
> *Professor of Strategy*
> *Ecole Superieure de Guerre*

> "Who the hell wants to hear actors talk?"
> *-HARRY M. WARNER*
> *Warner Bros., 1927*

> "I think there is a market for maybe five computers."
> *-THOMAS WATSON*
> *Chairman of IBM, 1943*

> "We don't like their sound, and guitar music is on the way out."
> *-DECCA RECORDING CO.*
> *Rejecting the Beatles, 1962*

> "There is no reason for any individuals to have a computer in their home."
> *-KEN OLSEN*
> *President, Chairman, & Founder*
> *Digital Equipment Corp., 1977*

Notice the dates these statements were made? We're talking about things that were said within the last century or so! One can find many other examples just as amusing as those listed above from various business and industry "experts" that have occurred as recently as the last decade or two. For those of you not in business or industry, don't get too smug because similar examples exist in every field and discipline, from academics to politics. For purposes of this book, I've made a conscious decision not to start quoting from politics or political leaders, which would be a whole book in itself! Maybe even several volumes!

Anticipating the unlimited discoveries and technological advances possible in the future, learning, challenging our paradigms, and having an open mind to change should prove to be exciting and rewarding adventures in themselves. Unfortunately for many people, and I could probably venture to say "most," their learning curves seem to level off very quickly upon reaching their mid-twenties, and in many cases a lot earlier. Scholars throughout history concur learning and self-improvement is a challenging and time consuming process, but agree in numbers it can also be a most rewarding endeavor.

There was a time in my early work career when I taught at the college level. Whether it was with undergraduates or graduate students, I noticed a unique and predictable phenomenon. Now keep in mind, college students are paying, or their parents are, for what's known as a "higher" education. I would assume, regardless of their specific motivations, students were there because they wanted to be in school to "better themselves" in some manner for the future. Maybe the objective was to prepare for a career or to take the time to explore, learn, and decide what to do with the rest of their lives. Whatever the reasons, the bottom line was they were purchasing a product, supposedly an education, and investing in themselves and their futures.

My agenda for the first day of class was usually a presentation of the course, course objectives, the grading system, all assignments for the semester, and my expectations of students to receive a passing grade. For any course I taught, my intention was to facilitate a stimulating environment for learning. My responsibility was to provide activities and learning experiences that would ignite independent interest and continued personal study in the discipline or a closely related field. Ninety-nine percent of the time on the first day of class, usually right after I held up the required book(s) for the semester, some of the first questions posed to me by the class would be "How many pages is it?" and "Will we have to read the whole thing?" When I replied the book had only four hundred fifty pages, and that yes, they would have to read the whole thing, I would hear a definite but subdued moan. The hushed moan usually swept from the front of the room to the back, almost as if the entire class was participating in a "verbal wave," but without standing or using their arms.

After the moaning and buzzing subsided, I would slowly scan the class and try to make eye contact with as many students as I could. Maybe direct eye contact would make some of them think I might be mean and excessively demanding during the semester and then they might consider dropping the class. What better way to pare down the size of the class especially since the university administration regularly managed to over-schedule and overbook the number of students registered not only for my classes, but all classes! Remember, colleges and universities are businesses and work off of budgets too! No matter how I tried though, my tactics rarely succeeded. Continuing with an exaggerated fake look of bewilderment and disgust on my face, I would ask in a very soft but direct voice, "Tell me, how many weeks are there in this semester?" Like the unified roar from the home team fans after a game-winning touchdown, I would hear the response, "Fifteen!" Next, as I was nodding my head in approval and agreement with their reply, I would ask who the mathematics majors were in the class. After a few hands would go in the air, and my head still nodding approval, I would ask the entire class to divide four hundred fifty by fifteen. The majority of the class still wasn't sure of where I was going with my questions, but they would real soon. Again the class would respond in unison, "Thirty!"

"Okay, now I have one more math problem for you to calculate," still nodding my head, "What's the answer if you divide thirty by six?" By now, the array of non-verbals and puzzled looks on the students' faces was always amusing. The class would respond in chorus, which now seemed scripted, and I would continue by repeating their answer, "Five! Congratulations, that's exactly correct. Now, considering I'll give you Sundays off, that leaves six study days per week available throughout the semester when you can devote at least some time to reading for this class. Now, how many of you can't read five pages a day for this class?" It's an old sales technique called "minimizing," just like marketers and advertisers use when they tell you it costs only "pennies a day" for their product or service. At this point I wouldn't hear any more moans or groans, nor did I ever see anyone raise his hand indicating he couldn't read those five pages a day. I always assumed the silence from the class was an indication they were pondering and seriously considering purchasing and reading additional books from the "Optional Reading List" attached to the class syllabus. I can fantasize too, can't I? I always attached an "Optional Reading List" as part of my first-day-of-class tactics to scare students into reconsidering dropping the class.

After almost a decade in the academic world, I made the transition and crossed that bridge into the "corporate" business world. Naturally, some of my habits from academics carried over with me, one of which was to read at least one book a week. When I say a book, I'm referring to a text or something that might be listed on the *Business Week* top ten list, in addition to reading various weekly and monthly magazines. Shortly after joining the ranks of "corporate" America, I was reading about a research study that presented some very startling and personally eye-opening statistics. The research found *less* than one in ten American managers and employees had completely read a book or text pertaining to his work or career over the previous year. From the research, that number was true for both new and seasoned employees. Needless to say, I wasn't only shocked, but amazed as well. Being the inquisitive type, I started to unscientifically conduct my own field research. Regularly I would ask other "corporate" colleagues about books they might have read over the past year or so. Also, when I made presentations at various meetings, I made it a habit to ask for a show of hands from those who had completely read "one" book over the past year. As a number of hands would rise, I would then clarify my question by stating that the reading had to be on a topic related to their career or vocation. Most hands went down. Guess what? My numbers validated and to this day continue to support the research!

One of the annual requirements I have for all my direct reports is they read at least two books or texts related to their work and company assignments. Not articles or pamphlets, but a recent text or business book related to their jobs or fields of expertise. It could be in anything from project management, supervising employees, change management, to whatever they might be interested in at the time, so long as it pertained to their jobs in some way. At first I would get the typical resistance and excuses why such an assignment would be impossible to accomplish over the next year. I would listen to the excuses for about one minute, because that's just about how long it took before they didn't know what else to say without repeating themselves! Generally their excuses were without substance. Then I would inform them I was making a unilateral management decision. Reading two books over the next year would be incorporated as part of their performance review requirements and objectives for the upcoming year. Just as I did in the collegiate world, I would explain that most business books average between one hundred fifty to three hundred pages. Excluding weekends, holidays, and vacations, they have approximately two hundred twenty-five workdays a year available to them. Notice I said *work* days! Then I would ask the question, "Would it be asking too much of you to read approximately two pages a day?" I even went so far as to suggest they take the first five minutes of *every workday* as they drink their morning coffee, to close their doors and dedicate the first cup of coffee and "paid" five minutes to reading. I never got much resistance at that point in the conversation. After about six months of encouraging and individually discussing some of the books they were reading, the easiest part of the following year's performance reviews was their reading, learning, and self improvement objectives. The five minutes of

Personal Values

daily reading generally expanded to ten, fifteen, or even thirty minutes over time, usually at their discretion.

Talk about a very simple, effective, and inexpensive corporate-wide competitive advantage to implement! Suppose all managers and employees in your organization read two books a year related to their jobs or your business. I'll guarantee within two years your workforce will be head and shoulders above your competition. The books or texts could be assigned on a company-wide basis, could be employee specific, or both. A five-minute daily investment for a lifetime of returns!

Daniel R. Burr was the VP for Training and Development for the corporation. When I joined the company, I had little occasion or reason to interact with him. It wasn't intentional; it was just our roles and responsibilities took us in different directions. Besides, he worked out of an office in another part of the country. If his name ever did come up in casual conversation around the office, people would usually change the subject, bring up another name, or if pressured, say something profound like, "Oh, Dan, right. I met him." Then they would casually, but deliberately, change the subject. That reaction was universal among a majority of my "corporate" colleagues.

With such a consistent and predictable response, my curiosity was raised about this Dan guy. Periodically I would ask a few trusted colleagues, in private, why they reacted the way they did when Dan's name was brought up. Before changing the subject, their responses generally boiled down to, "He's a *different* kind of person!" or "He's a little *strange*." When I would pursue their definition of "different" or "strange," just a little further, they always had a difficult time coming up with an answer, or they would again say something profound like, "You know." I eventually came to the conclusion their answers and discomfort with Dan revolved around his inability to interact and socialize with others. Their answers about his behavior and mannerisms were quickly rationalized because, as they would say, he was "one of those intellectual types." Talk about someone who was an enigma...

By coincidence, Dan and I formally met each other while attending one of the few company-sponsored management training programs hosted by the "corporate" training and development department. The particular two-day program we attended in Chicago was entitled *Change Leadership.* The internally developed program was facilitated by a twenty-two-year-old woman. She had recently completed her Master's Degree program just prior to joining the company. With limited, less than two months to be exact, platform and facilitation skills, not to mention any prior business experience, the trainer faced a tough training task and a less than receptive audience. But remembering the quote from Anna Freud, *"Creative minds always have been known to survive any kind of bad training,"* I looked forward to the program with anticipation. Besides, I've never met anyone I haven't learned something from.

I could never understand why corporate trainers feel obligated to schedule every last minute for the program participants, including the *mandatory* evening dinner. The featured sampling of local cuisine at these training programs was usually served at some crowded and noisy local restaurant. Somehow, Dan and I were assigned adjacent dinner seats, which expedited our first face-to-face introduction to each other. Can you imagine assigned seats for an informal evening dinner with other "corporate" managers? What will trainers think of next? After a casual handshake, better known as the *"introduction,"* Dan started applying and demonstrating his mastery of the seven steps of making a sales call during our dinner conversation. He smoothly transitioned into sales call step number two, *"developing rapport."* Dan must have known

Personal Values

I started my career in the world of higher education because he suddenly asked, "Bryan, I understand you were a college professor at one time? Where and what did you teach?"

After we exchanged and shared our abbreviated bios, Dan asked me what I'd thought of the day's training session. I didn't know at the time the program instructor reported to Dan. Being diplomatic, and also remembering my first year in front of bloodthirsty graduate students, I said I would reserve my comments until the program was over the next day. Of course Dan didn't know I would have to rush to the airport the next day to catch a flight. All participants had been informed that scheduling early departures was "unacceptable," but they didn't say we couldn't leave the exact minute the program was scheduled to be over. Because of the way the seating and tables were arranged, Dan and I were captive audiences for each other throughout the evening, which lasted about three hours.

My earlier assumptions were correct, Dan didn't possess the greatest of social skills, but he sure seemed to be well-read and versed on many topics. As we talked, I was impressed with some of the "buzz" words he was casually using and throwing around. He was starting to sound like some of my former colleagues at the university. I'm not sure if it was for my benefit or whether it was his normal modus operandi, but he would mention specific authors of recently published business books, many of which I'd read. For the first hour or so we briefly touched on about fifteen different topics, all of which seemed to be in vogue at the time. Of those fifteen or so, several were topics I had a personal interest in, like customer service, value chains, and customer-driven marketing. Not only was I interested in the subjects, but coincidentally several of my upcoming projects focused on those topics. Dan appeared to be someone I might want to use as a sounding board for some of my thoughts, maybe even to serve as an informal "coach" for me. I'm always in search of good coaches and mentors. What a resource! He could probably provide me with some constructive feedback or guidance. To date, I hadn't met anyone else within the company who was so well-read or seemed to have a genuine interest in *my* topics.

I was impressed with Dan's unique ability to ask the right questions, summarize topics, and with how he showed a sincere interest in talking with me. We never ventured into much detail on any one particular subject that night, but it was probably just as well because of the situation and all the different restaurant distractions. Several times Dan said he had an interest in talking more, and that he would like to get together again in the near future so we could do just that. He said something about finding me like a "breath of fresh air" compared to a lot of people he worked with in the company. I'm not sure what he meant by that comment, but on the other hand, who wouldn't appreciate such flattery? Even though his speech and mannerisms were very distracting, not to mention his thick glasses that looked like "Coke bottle bottoms," I was looking forward to that opportunity. The sooner the better!

It was about ten days after returning to the office from the training program Dan showed up. He intentionally extended his regularly scheduled monthly trip to the "corporate" office by one day so we could get together. After consulting with and getting approval from my wife, I decided to invite Dan over to our home for an evening dinner and the opportunity to talk without distractions. Considering our discussions were probably not going to be limited entirely to work-related topics, but probably more Socratic in nature, the relaxed atmosphere of a family room and a bottle of wine seemed appropriate.

Just before we got to the main course, after enjoying a fine Caesar salad, which by the way, included a coddled egg mixed in, I started to notice a prevailing trend in our conversation. It seems we would jump from topic to topic never getting into

Personal Values

much depth on any one of them. Maybe it was just Dan's comfort level, considering he was a first-time dinner guest at a colleague's home and wasn't sure of their tastes and interests. Under the circumstances, he was probably feeling a little on the spot. Besides, why would he want to get into a major philosophical discussion, not knowing for sure if my wife would be interested in such esoteric things?

By dessert, I was dying to share my thoughts and solicit insights from Dan on some of the things I'd wanted to talk about all evening, like customer service, market orientation, and value chains. From our discussions at the restaurant earlier in the month, I knew he would be a wealth of knowledge, not to mention the possibility of filling the role of personal coach and mentor along the way. Now was my time!

One of the books Dan mentioned at the training session was going to be the basis of a new and innovative project I was working on for the company. When I mentioned the book's title, Dan quickly said the author's name and indicated it was a good reference and thought provoking book. Wonderful, I thought!

There was one long chapter in the book, chapter eleven, that particularly intrigued me, and I was curious about Dan's thoughts on it. When I asked him about his impressions and the applicability of the concepts presented in that chapter to our company, Dan got a blank look on his face. Okay, it was probably one of those chapters that hadn't caught Dan's interest. But before I could refresh his memory and summarize the chapter in a sentence or two, you know, just to jog his thought processes, Dan said in a subdued voice, "I haven't actually read that book yet. I only read a book review on it in one of those flight magazines about a month or so ago, just before our training session in Chicago. But I do have it on my reading list."

I'm good at picking up on these types of subtle hints. A little disappointed, I figured I should move on to another topic! When we were at the training session, I specifically remembered Dan talking at dinner about a book he'd recently read on organizational change. I'd just finished reading that same book, based solely on his positive recommendation at the seminar. What better way to salvage what seemed to be an uncomfortable situation for Dan, and my wife and me for that matter, than to bring up a topic I thought he had a passion for, and a book he'd already read. What happened next played out like a dramatic scene intended for a low budget movie entitled *True Confessions.* Dan sheepishly said he hadn't really read that book either. Instead, he'd listened to the condensed executive series version of it on audiotape. He went on to say, no let's change that to confess, that because of his schedule, he doesn't have the luxury of doing all the reading he'd like to do. In an attempt to save face, he did interject he religiously listens to condensed audio books while driving, and regularly reads the one-page business book reviews in *Business Week* and airline flight magazines.

From that point on, the remainder of the evening was dedicated to conversations about wine, television, music, and food. Such topics generally lend themselves well to "safe" extended conversation about one's personal tastes and opinions. They were definitely "safe" topics! How could anyone dispute the fact that a '91 Merlot is different from a '92 Pinot Noir, or rap music has a different beat than country and western!

After Dan left that evening, my wife Wendy and I both enjoyed another glass of wine. It was a glass of *Pisano* poured from a screw top gallon jug. As we privately debriefed and laughed about the evening with Dan, we mutually came to the conclusion he would not be included in the top 95% of people on our "to be invited back" list. My wife concluded Dan had a disproportionate balance between his "breadth and depth of

Personal Values

knowledge," heavy on the "breadth" but *real, real* shallow on the "depth."

Is that what everyone else meant when they said Dan was one of those "intellectual types?"

In Dan's case, maybe a corollary to the saying *"The more you know, the more you know you don't know!"* might better be stated as *"The more Dan seems to know, the more you realize he doesn't know!"*

Chapter XV

Never Enough Time...

> *Then be not coy, but use your time;*
> *And while ye may, go marry:*
> *For having list but once your prime,*
> *You may for ever tarry.*
> *Herrick 1591-1674*

Have you ever heard the axiom, *"You never seem to have enough time to do it right the first time, but you always have the time to do it over."* I think the first time I heard that saying, or at least the first time it seemed to make sense to me, was after I joined the official ranks of American taxpayers. That practical saying seems to be a corollary to another familiar saying related to the various *"quality"* movements in American business and industry. That maxim is simply stated as *"Do it right the first time."*

After reviewing the different directions and emphases (or maybe we can better characterize them as fads) over the sixty plus year history of the American "quality control movement," they all had generally the same goal. That objective was to

Personal Values

move from the ineffectiveness and high costs of *"defect detection"* to the lower cost benefits of *"defect prevention."* Sampling plans were the thing in the 1950s. The 1960s introduced many "zero defect" initiatives. The "people" side of the equation took over in the 1970s with quality circles, a concept imported from Japan. The 1980s emphasized statistical process control and control charts. It seems you couldn't walk into any business in the 1980s without seeing control charts plastered over the walls, ceilings, floors, and the front-page headlines of company newsletters. The 1990s embraced the implementation of the principles of total quality management, better known by the acronym, TQM. We'll have to wait a few more years to characterize the first decade of the twenty-first century. The quality movement over the decades has generally focused on the basic principle of "doing it right the first time."

Maybe it was my generation, the era when I grew up, the idiosyncrasies of small town U.S.A., or even the fluoride in the water, but our concentration and attention spans seemed longer than children of today. Research backs up that statement, indicating children today do have shorter attention spans than children did just two short decades ago. The studies didn't address intelligence or knowledge, just attention spans. So I'm not implying about how "smart" children were in my day or are now. Maybe as kids back in the fifties, we weren't cognizant enough to realize it, but we didn't have the "sensory overload" in our lives kids now seem to have. Sure, we had television back then, but we could get only three channels, not the two hundred plus channels now beamed into a majority of American homes. Did you realize it takes at least sixteen and two-thirds minutes each time you methodically surf those two hundred channels? And that's assuming you spend just five seconds previewing each channel. Figure it out, two hundred channels times five seconds each equals one thousand seconds. Divide those one thousand seconds by sixty seconds per minute and the result is sixteen and two-thirds minutes. Now keep in mind, I didn't factor in other potential channel surfing delays like waiting for commercials or pausing to see if a particular program looks interesting enough to watch. Decisions! Decisions! Decisions! How many times a week do you channel surf?

Just a generation ago, we didn't have computers and electronic games, extensive organized sports, and all the other distractions that now compete for the time and attention of both children and adults. I'm sure we drove our parents just as crazy as kids do today, but somehow it was at a different level.

One of my passions as a kid was building models. It didn't matter if the models were of cars, airplanes, ships, or those see-through replicas of the human body. I loved making models, whether from unassembled pre-fabricated kits, plans, or self-designed ideas. Using artist's terms, my *medium* was anything from plastic, paper and balsa wood, to the amateur engineer's version of an *Erector Set*. I still have that *Erector Set* packed somewhere in a box in the attic. I would find myself spending hours upon hours engrossed in designing and building the "perfect" model. No, the amount of time spent had nothing to do with my limited mental capabilities, as my sisters jokingly but continually claimed, sometimes even to this day.

My philosophy back then was fairly simple. *If it's worth doing at all, do it right!"* Not far removed from the idea of *"Doing it right the first time."* Naturally, I was the one who determined what "right" meant. Once I remember building a model airplane, whose frame and superstructure was constructed of balsa wood, covered with a special kind of paper, and then eventually sealed and painted. Now that might not sound like a major challenge to some of you aeronautical types, but the plans I followed required drawing and cutting over one thousand five hundred individual parts from flat balsa wood stock. Did I mention the wingspan was fifty-four inches? By comparison, the wing span was wider than I was tall. The Concord probably wasn't even on the drawing boards yet. Today, grade school kids the same age as I was then, are able to apply computer-aided drafting and computer aided manufacturing techniques, better known as CAD/CAM, to do the same thing I did, but in virtual reality. My pride came from producing a model that was extremely well designed and masterfully crafted, even down to the internal parts that would never be seen. The amount of time I spent varied from model to model, but work on the models was never rushed nor were corners cut just to get it done. Quality to me was a mindset. Every piece and process was meticulously executed so there were no flaws anywhere in the final product. For me, it was a matter of pride when friends would visit and I could proudly show off "my works of art."

For whatever reason, that personal pride was instilled in me at a very early age and was continually demonstrated in just about everything I did, whether it was hobbies, schoolwork assignments, or washing the family car on Saturdays. Notice I did say "just about everything." There were some things I despised doing. As a little boy, I was always interested in cars and trucks, so when I washed the family car, I took great pride in having thoroughly cleaned both the interior and exterior. The tires were well scrubbed and all doorjambs wiped clean. The interior was vacuumed and floor mats precisely placed to cover the holes in the floorboards. Back then I gave new meaning to the term "detailed." Surprisingly, as a would-be entrepreneur, I had a thriving car washing business during warmer weather. Neighbors scheduled me in advance to wash their cars and they usually tipped very well, over and above my standard charges for my services. Never once did I receive a complaint about not meeting their expectations, probably because they paid me substantially less than what it would have cost them at the commercial car wash. Washing dishes on the other hand was a task I despised. Thank goodness for two older sisters!

Even to this day, taking pride in and having the reputation for "doing things right" is a goal I constantly strive for. It's not always easy, but the benefits have been priceless over the long haul. When I think back and wonder if there was one significant event in my life that instilled the "do it right the first time" mentality, there isn't anything I can specifically point to. My sisters also had and still have the same tendency, but, from my biased perspective, not to the same extent as I do. Generally I attribute it to our parents, their guidance, and high, but realistic, expectations of us. Reinforcement and support received from friends and other acquaintances also contributed to that sense of pride and self esteem.

Robert Wolber had been with the company for a total of twenty-one years, though not all of them consecutive years. He'd left the company after about twelve years to work in an unrelated field then returned to this company nine years ago. Robert seems to have a way with people. Anybody and everybody associates well with him, similar to the way little children relate and interact with their well-intentioned and loving grandparents. Grandparents can violate any number of family rules, and generally get away with it, or at a minimum be tolerated in a positive way. After spoiling their grandchildren during a visit, grandparents can return the kids back to their parents all wound-up tighter than a watch-spring. It's true, grandchildren are parents' sweet revenge on their children. Not that Robert is a grandfather that we're aware of, at least not yet, but he has that same uncanny ability to fit in wherever he goes. What a charmer! As a Product Marketing Manager over his entire career, he's had the opportunity to associate or work with just about everyone inside the company, in addition to having had extensive interactions with most customers. Whenever Robert's name was brought up, people would generally say, like they did about so many others in the company, "he's really dedicated and easy to work with."

Robert and I seemed to hit it off from the first day we met. With only a few years separating us in age, we seemed to have similar backgrounds and interests. That's probably why we enjoyed talking about almost anything and everything. He was well-read and we enjoyed arguing just for the sake of argument. Not in an adversarial or hostile way, but more like politicians sparing on the floor of the House of Representatives or Senate, then both enjoying a social drink together that same evening. Notice I didn't mention any specific names of politicians! Robert must have gained some of his experience from competing on his high school and college debating teams. Many times I thought to myself he would make a "good" politician, and I told him so. Once he admitted there were times, but very few, when he thought he'd missed his calling and should have gone into politics when he was younger. We never did talk, though, about what he thought makes a "good" politician. I reserve my opinions on that topic, too.

One of the first projects we worked on together, after I joined the company, was coordinating an annual focus group comprised of a number of "critical" customers. "Critical" in this case meant they purchased a lot of product from our company. "Critical" was the only criteria used to select the focus group members. Who cared if they had anything to contribute or not? To add credibility to the focus group process, and encourage those "critical" customers, who were invited to participate and hopefully made to think they were considered special, the focus group was designated the official sounding title of "The Corporate Advisory Forum." Other perks for participating "Forum" members included several all-expense paid days at a plush resort. In an effort to impress, included were things like first-class air transportation, sometimes via the corporate jet (if they were "critical" enough), golf or some other recreation of their choice, meals prepared by an internationally known chef, and memorabilia such as shirts, hats, and jackets with our company logo embroidered on each. At times it looked like we were producing walking advertisements instead of soliciting customer input. The participants went home with practically a complete new wardrobe. In return for such extravagance, personal amenities, and mementos, the participants agreed to provide their "honest and candid feedback" to a number of pre-determined questions during the meetings. Our management team usually knew what they wanted the Forum participants to say even before they said it. And if they didn't say what was expected, our management team would ignore or casually overlook their comments. The feedback usually happened in roundtable format with several of our "corporate" managers and executives taking notes on their personalized "corporate" letterhead tablets. Having "corporate" letterhead paper with your individual name and official title embossed on the top was another one of those executive status symbols in our company. What better place to show off than with our "critical" customers?

Robert, reporting through Bob Spencer, (You remember him, don't you?) the VP for Marketing, had been assigned the task of coordinating The Corporate Advisory Forum for the last several years. The VP of Marketing always provided what he thought was his valued input to the coordinating group, but remained at arm's length from the actual work and planning process, at least until everyone arrived at the resort. Politically, that was a very smart thing to do; at least he thought so. If things were progressing well, he'd take credit for the entire event. On the other hand, if things were a little less than organized or feedback from the customers was less than stellar, he had a very interesting way of removing himself from the process and placing blame on Robert and the planning committee. Bob Spencer was that kind of political animal, but you already know about him from some earlier chapters.

Robert scheduled the first meeting of "The Advisory Forum Planning Committee" approximately five months before the anticipated event. Considering the amount of work and coordination needed to be done, it seemed wise and the sign of a prudent manager to start early. Eight minutes after the scheduled time for the meeting, Robert distributed the agenda to everyone in the room. After a number of opening remarks from several of the committee members and a quick summary of last year's Forum meeting participant feedback, Robert read through the agenda so everyone would be able to understand what it contained. His original copy of the agenda, which was in his own handwriting, appeared to have been written while driving in stop-and-go traffic in downtown Los Angeles during rush hour. Now let's agree on one thing. If you're like me, which Robert is, our combined handwriting skills are similar to ancient hieroglyphics even the FBI couldn't decipher. When written on what appeared to be parchment from colonial America or more likely the greasy wrapper from a Big Mac, and subsequently reproduced on a copier that needed its ink cartridge recharged, the outcome was obvious. The agenda Robert distributed to each committee member would have served better as recycled napkins and place mats for the box of bagels sitting in the middle of the conference table.

At the second meeting, held only one week later, we essentially completed the planning process and committed it to paper. How could we do it so quickly? We were just repeating what was done last year! We even started some implementation procedures, including activities, specific dates, and confirmed reservations at the resort. As part of his assignment from the previous week, Robert distributed a copy of the invitation letter he'd already forwarded to all those who were on this year's invitation list. At first glance, the letter had face appeal. The body of the letter was well-spaced with left and right margin justification. The printing was well-balanced and centered between the header and footer on the "corporate" stationery. It was obvious Robert was proud and pleased with himself as he announced that within several of the paragraphs, he intentionally personalized the contents for each of the individual recipients. He even included handwritten notes on the bottom of several invitations, just to convey the impression to the recipient they were *special* to the company. And why not? Considering "The Corporate Advisory Forum" members represented our "critical" accounts, wasn't it necessary to make them feel special and appreciated?

The first paragraph of the letter started out as follows:

> *I am pleased to invite you the 5th Anal Corporate Advisory Forum. This year we will be meeting at the the Executive Conference Resort and Gulf Club. Mark your calendars now for October. As in past years, your participation and input provides us input to better serve you, our wanderful customers!*

As the planning committee started to read the letter, it took approximately thirteen seconds before Jennifer Dorney raised the first question. "Robert, has this letter *already* been sent to each of the invited guests?" She emphasized the word "already." The stunned looks of amazement from the rest of the group quickly spread across the room. They all raised their eyes from what appeared to be very focused reading.

Robert proudly said, "They sure have! I personally dropped them off at the post office last night on my way home from the office."

Jennifer missed her calling as an actress for a TV sitcom. In her expressive but sarcastic "wife" role, she asked Robert if his computer had a key on it for "spell check." His response was, "I think so. Why do you ask?" Without answering, Jennifer offered to proofread *any* future correspondence *before* it went out.

Over the next few months, the regularly scheduled planning meetings progressed quite well. From most of the verbal progress reports, it seemed everyone was getting his assignment(s) done on time and things were shaping up with what appeared to be very few loose ends.

One of the benefits of serving on the Planning Committee was the opportunity to arrive at the resort a day or so early. Several committee members took the "day or so" literally. You know, just to take care of any of those loose ends that might arise. The round of golf right after we arrived was integral to the success of the meeting! This orientation to the course prepared us to play less-obvious "customer golf." Having at least some familiarity with the links, we could individually plan and subsequently play our *poor* shots intentionally.

As we arrived en masse at the front desk reception area of the resort, the banquet and special events director greeted us. Her name was Claudia. With a very professional demeanor, she asked if Robert Wolber was with us, stating she needed to speak with him. Robert quickly came forward as she opened a small expandable portfolio she carried at her side. Extending her hand to greet Robert, she said in a soft but direct tone, "Mr. Wolber, nice to finally meet you in person. We've been having difficulty getting in touch with you over the past several weeks. There are a few minor details we need to review immediately. Could we possibly do that now?" Off they went to Claudia's office, not to be seen until the rest of us gathered at the nineteenth hole, about four and a half hours later.

Never Enough Time...

When Robert joined us in the outdoor lounge, we asked if everything was under control with Claudia, making a few innuendoes in the process. Appearing a little embarrassed, Robert said there had been a few *minor* details to sort out, which he and Claudia did. It had been a grueling day on the links under the blazing sun, so the refreshments and complementary food bar were a big hit. Even though Robert didn't play golf that afternoon, his presence on the course wasn't missed. But he sure made up for it in the lounge, especially at the food bar. Piling on as many jumbo shrimp as a small appetizer plate can hold, Robert casually mentioned that the next day's dinner menu had been changed. Instead of the originally planned *"live lobster and seafood festival"* for the following night's dinner, Robert informed us he had to change the main course selection. It seems Robert hadn't sent the dinner selections the committee agreed on to the resort on time. Actually, Robert forgot to send them altogether. Unfortunately, it takes more than twenty-four hours to fly in *live* lobsters, so steak, baked potatoes, and vegetables would have to do.

Other than three invited guests having to commission a taxi from the airport to the resort, because they hadn't been informed about the limo transfer arrangements, everyone arrived without incident. The meeting started the next morning right on time. However, the confusion and distraction of passing around just one magic marker for all participants to print their names on their table name tents and badges was a little awkward. The paper clips securing the agenda and various other papers including the roster of attendees, golf rules, departure instructions, and program evaluation forms, by mid-morning served wonderfully for cleaning under fingernails and picking teeth. Robert apologized for the unprofessional appearance of the handouts, and then assured everyone name-embossed leather portfolios would be sent to each of the participants in about a week. Seems the order was

Personal Values

placed late (last week) with the vendor and even with a last minute rush order request, the vendor was still stretching to get them delivered by the week following our meeting.

The meeting progressed as well as could be expected. Considering the guests, who were our "critical" customers and were, in many cases, direct competitors with each other, what's the likelihood of us getting candid and honest feedback? Would you discuss business problems you might be experiencing, especially with your competitor sitting across the table listening with eyes and ears wide open, pen in hand, scribbling pages of notes? The presence of a good attorney might also have been advisable given some of the topics that were on the table. I understand if one is found guilty of collusion and price fixing, the consequences can be rather serious, as well as having a potential long-term negative impact on the business.

On the last day of the meeting, every one of us on the Planning Committee declined the invitation to get in front of the group to present a small gift and token of the company's appreciation to each of the participants. Robert again came to the plate! Each participant was to be presented a golf shirt and a windbreaker jacket. Each garment was embroidered with a professionally designed logo/graphic and the words "Corporate Advisory Forum." The shirts and jackets looked great! The graphic was done in colors that blended very well with the background colors and fabric. I wouldn't venture to guess the exact cost of those promotional items, but it was obvious from their feel and quality, they didn't come from the local recycled or thrift store. As Robert made the announcement that each participant would receive his or her own shirt and jacket, he proudly held up a sample of each. With the unopened boxes of apparel conspicuously stacked in the corner of the meeting room, Robert continued with his closing remarks and words of appreciation for their time and valuable contributions to the meeting. His last sentence before wishing them a safe trip home was, "On the sheet of paper that's being passed around, please write your name, shirt size, and jacket size. Seems all those boxes over there in the corner are sized 'extra small.' We'll send you your correct size in about two weeks. Thank you for attending!"

Three weeks after the "Corporate Advisory Forum" meeting, I helped Robert load his truck with approximately fifty boxes containing individually packaged shirts and jackets. Robert was glad to get them out of his office, and the clerk at FedEx was equally pleased her company was selected as the carrier of choice. While riding shotgun as Robert drove to the FedEx office, I listened to him go into an extended litany about how Bob Spencer, his boss, called him on the carpet about not attending to the details while planning and implementing the Corporate Advisory Forum meeting. About half an hour into the meeting Bob Spencer strategically positioned himself as having nothing to do with the organization or planning of the meeting, other than as an invited representative of the company. Robert said Bob was, in Bob's own words, "Rather disappointed that there were a number of obvious loose ends in the planning and execution of the meeting." According to Bob, a majority of the attendees indicated the same sentiment on their evaluation forms. All of the "loose ends," as Bob called them, were Robert's direct responsibility; no other Planning Committee member was implicated in any way, at least according to Robert.

On the way back to the office from FedEx, Robert said that with all of his other responsibilities and work, he hadn't been able to find the time to attend to *all* those "minor" and "incidental" details, even though he'd initially agreed to take responsibility for them. "Everyone still had a good time anyway, didn't they?" he asked.

Personal Values

Just when I was about to respond to his question with some philosophical answer that would avoid his real question, Robert continued by saying Bob Spencer gave him a number of specific suggestions on how to improve on next year's Corporate Advisory Forum Meeting. Seems Bob already assigned Robert the responsibility for next year's extravaganza!

I didn't need to say a thing as we pulled into the parking lot and quickly jumped out of the truck. That old saying came to my mind as we parted company at the entrance to the building. *"You never have enough time to do it right the first time, but you always have the time to do it over."*

It looks like Robert has approximately three hundred forty days to do it over...

Chapter XVI

I Value My Garden...

I value my garden more for being full of blackbirds than of cherries, and very frankly give them fruit for their songs.

Joseph Addison 1672-1719

It's the last chapter, so why not start it off with a last chapter definition! This book focused on individual or personal, and collective "values," which are *beliefs, standards* and *philosophical convictions.* According to Webster's Dictionary, "ethics" is defined as *"the principles of conduct governing an individual or a group."* Doubleday Dictionary similarly defines "ethics" as *"the basic principles of right action."* How often it is that we observe incongruity between another person's values and his behaviors! How often do we see the same incongruity between our own values and actions?

What child hasn't tried his hand at gardening? For most of us, it probably wasn't working several acres, but more like a few small pots, a planter, or a small plot of dirt. For those who were really ambitious, a garden of a hundred square feet or so fit the bill. That's only an area ten feet by ten feet! One spring, after a unanimous vote around the dinner table, my sisters and I decided that a "kids" family garden was necessary to provide all sorts of "free" vegetables and fresh produce for the family, relatives, and community in general. Mom and Dad humored us, well aware of what the outcome would probably be by harvest time. We had visions of *"amber waves of grain"* and *"corn as high as an elephant's eye"* as the three of us planned the crops to be cultivated and the plot layout. In reality, my oldest sister orchestrated most of the plans and unilaterally made all the decisions. Work assignments were semi-negotiated, while discussions of annual crop rotations and how to work the futures market were incorporated as part of our business plan. Our first draft, accompanied by elaborate drawings for the proposed garden would have required a minimum of three hundred fifty acres, to accommodate what we had planned and anticipated accomplishing. Fortunately, Dad convinced us a fifteen- by fifteen-foot section on the family's fifty-four acres of land might be a little more realistic. At first we were reluctant to accept his suggestion, but later agreed to his proposal, especially after he offered to do the initial tilling of the soil.

With strings stretched as guidelines between strategically surveyed marker sticks, the individual seeds were tenderly and carefully planted to the exact envelope recommendations for depth and spacing. We had enough string stretched in various directions across our garden that a neighbor suggested we start our own fabric weaving operation as a sideline. Corn was planted in row one, followed by beans, then onions, sunflowers, carrots, lettuce, pumpkins, watermelons, and tomatoes. The order of the crops was decided by consensus and what we thought the "perfect" fully-grown garden would look like. We gave little consideration to growth patterns or shade from neighboring crops. We also read somewhere in a seed catalog that marigolds planted around the perimeter of a garden would keep rabbits out.

Slightly after sunrise the day after planting, we couldn't wait to race to the garden and admire the fruits of our previous day's labor. To our disappointment, nothing appeared to be growing. With some guidance and encouragement from our parents we were finally convinced the garden wasn't dead, it just needed a little more time and nurturing. With constant and dedicated vigilance, along with our daily dose of gardening TLC (tender loving care), we started to see a few new plants pushing up through the soil. We learned rather quickly that immediate gratification and gardening didn't go together, at least when it comes to harvesting ripe vegetables and other produce. We experienced several emotional highs and lows during the first few weeks after planting. The highs came with seeing little plants pushing their tender green shoots up through the soil, the lows were the result of agonizingly slow growth rates. This farming stuff sure proved to be a little more difficult than we originally anticipated. Some of the hybrid weeds we were growing could have won first place ribbons at the county fair.

I can't tell you how many times the topic of "patience is a virtue" came up around the dinner table when we talked about the garden.

We didn't immediately realize it at the time, but rewards from the garden started well before anything edible, what little there was, appeared at our kitchen table. The array of wildlife the garden attracted was overwhelming. Deer, rabbits, birds, skunks, groundhogs, and just about every other animal Western Pennsylvania had to offer, visited "our" garden. Without understanding the concept at the time, we practiced organic farming before it was the politically correct thing to do. I don't think "safe" and environmentally friendly herbicides and insecticides were even developed then. Fencing and netting was a financial consideration the three of us kids didn't have the resources to invest in without considering a "farm" loan. My oldest sister convinced us the community bank wouldn't lend us money for capital improvements, like fencing, and our parents would probably charge the three of us exorbitant interest rates. After calculating how the costs of fencing would minimally impact our bottom line, our decision was easy. Fertilizing fell under the same category as the fencing. None of us particularly enjoyed gathering or spreading manure from other parts of our farm or the neighbor's farm, so our fertilizing efforts were kept to a bare minimum.

By mid-summer we named all the rabbits, along with the deer and groundhogs. We found it extremely difficult naming and remembering all the hundreds of birds that considered our garden their daily mealtime buffet. At first the visiting animals were viewed as pests, but after a few weeks they became the focal point of our garden.

We didn't quite get the yields we anticipated earlier in the spring, at least from our crops, but we did benefit from the experience more than we ever imagined, and in ways we never anticipated.

Hopefully, this book helped to plant a few new seeds in your garden of life. As we continuously cultivate the various rows of our own personal values, like integrity, honesty, truth, trust, creativity, learning, belief, excellence, responsibility, accountability, teamwork, or any of the other value seeds important in our personal and business lives, the yields can and will be priceless. Just as each individual seed contributes to the overall garden, all of our individual values and value systems contribute to our personal ethical character. Taking it one step further, our individual ethical character contributes to the betterment of all those we live with, interact with, work with, and to society in general.

Throughout the preceding chapters, I've presented a number of scenarios most of you can identify with, triggering personal memories from *your* childhood or adult and work life. The foundation for our values is developed in our youth and, like the garden, needs regular attention and nurturing throughout our lives.

Applying the p*rinciples of <u>right</u> <u>action</u>* and <u>*conduct*</u> based on a sound foundation of <u>*personal values*</u> will provide a bountiful life full of many unexpected rewards.

I would like to close with one more short, but thought provoking story:

One day a motivational speaker and "expert" in time management was speaking to a large group of business managers and, to drive home a point, used an illustration those managers will never forget.

As he stood in front of the gathering of high-powered over-achievers he said, "Okay, it's now time for a quiz." He carefully pulled out a one-gallon wide-mouthed glass jar hidden under the lectern and placed it on the table in front of him for everyone to see. Then he produced about a dozen fist-sized rocks and carefully placed them, one by one, into the jar. When the jar was filled to the top and no more rocks would fit inside, he asked, "Is the jar full?"

Everyone in the class said in unison, "Yes."

Then the speaker said in a questioning voice, "Really?"

He reached under the lectern again and pulled out a small pail full of gravel. Then he dumped some gravel into the larger jar and shook it, causing pieces of the gravel to work down into the spaces between the big rocks. Then he asked the attentive audience once more, "Is the jar full?"

By this time the class was on to him. "Probably not," one of them answered.

"Good!" he replied.

He reached under the lectern again and brought out a bucket of sand. He started pouring the sand in the jar and shaking it. The sand went into all the spaces left between the rocks and gravel. Once more he asked the question, "Is the jar full?"

"No!" the class shouted back.

Once again he said, "Good!"

Then he reached for a pitcher of water and began to pour it until the jar was filled to the brim. Then he looked at the class again and asked, "What is the point of this demonstration?"

One eager student raised his hand and said, "The point is, no matter how full your schedule is, if you try really hard you can always fit some more things in!"

"No!" the speaker replied, "that's not the point. The truth this illustration teaches us is if you don't put the big rocks in first, you'll never get them in at all. What are the 'big rocks' in your life? Your children... Your loved ones... Your education... Your dreams... A worthy cause... Teaching or mentoring others... Doing things you love... Time for yourself... Your health... Your significant other... Your career?"

I Value My Garden...

He continued, "Remember to put these BIG ROCKS in first or you'll never get them in at all. If you sweat the little stuff, the gravel, sand, and water, as in this demonstration, then you'll fill your life with little things to worry about that don't really matter, and you'll never have the quality time you need to spend on the big, important stuff, the *big rocks*."

So, tonight, or in the next day or so, when you're reflecting on this short story and this book in general, ask yourself this question:

> "What are the *big rocks*, or PERSONAL VALUES in my life?"

Then put those in your jar *first!*

Like the quote by Addison at the beginning of this chapter, I submit this book to you as *"...fruit for your songs."*

Epilogue:

If it be true that 'good wine needs no bush', tis true that a good play needs no epilogue.
Shakespeare 1564-1616

TO ORDER ADDITIONAL COPIES

Please Send the Following: **Qty.***   **Cost**

Personal Values: The Application   @ US $23.95   _____   _____
of Personal Values to the World
of Work
     Plus shipping and handling   @ $3 Standard   _____   _____
                                         ($5 Priority)

                                        TOTAL   _____

Phone Orders: 541.884.4818

FAX Orders: 541.884.4818

Mail This Form To: Pacific Press
                             P.O. Box 1965
                             Klamath Falls, Oregon 97601-0221

E-mail us at: pacificpress@performancesolution.com

Name:_____

Address:_____
_____

Phone:_____ FAX:_____

Payment: Visa_____ MasterCard_____

Print Name as it Appears on Card:_____

Card Number:_____

Exp. Date:_____ Cardholder's Signature:_____

ISBN 0-9678526-0-9   *Quantity Discounts Available*